New Normal, Radical Shift

New Normal, Radical Shift

Changing Business and Politics
for a Sustainable Future

NEELA BETTRIDGE
and
PHILIP WHITELEY

GOWER

© Neela Bettridge and Philip Whiteley 2013

All rights reserved. No part of this publication may be reproduced, stored in a retrieval system or transmitted in any form or by any means, electronic, mechanical, photocopying, recording or otherwise, without the prior permission of the publisher.

Published by
Gower Publishing Limited
Wey Court East
Union Road
Farnham
Surrey, GU9 7PT
England

Ashgate Publishing Company
110 Cherry Street
Suite 3-1
Burlington, VT 05401-3818
USA

www.gowerpublishing.com

Neela Bettridge and Philip Whiteley have asserted their moral right under the Copyright, Designs and Patents Act, 1988, to be identified as the authors of this work.

Gower Applied Business Research
Our programme provides leaders, practitioners, scholars and researchers with thought provoking, cutting edge books that combine conceptual insights, interdisciplinary rigour and practical relevance in key areas of business and management.

British Library Cataloguing in Publication Data
Bettridge, Neela.
  New normal, radical shift : changing business and politics
  for a sustainable future.
  1. Industrial management--Philosophy. 2. Business and
  politics. 3. Organizational change. 4. Business ethics.
  I. Title II. Whiteley, Philip.
  658'.001-dc23

Library of Congress Cataloging-in-Publication Data
Bettridge, Neela.
  New normal, radical shift : changing business and politics for a sustainable future / by Neela
  Bettridge and Philip Whiteley.
    p. cm.
  Includes bibliographical references and index.
  ISBN 978-1-4094-5574-5 (hbk) -- ISBN 978-1-4094-5575-2 (ebk) 1. Sustainable development.
  2. Social responsibility of business. 3. Corporate governance. 4. Leadership. 5. Organizational
  change. I. Whiteley, Philip. II. Title.
  HC79.E5B47 2013
  338.9'27--dc23

2012035594

ISBN 978 1 4094 5574 5 (hbk)
ISBN 978 1 4094 5575 2 (ebk – PDF)
ISBN 978 1 4724 0819 8 (ebk – ePUB)

Printed and bound in Great Britain by the
MPG Books Group, UK

CONTENTS

Reviews for

New Normal, Radical Shift
Changing Business and Politics
for a Sustainable Future

It would be easy to conclude that today's economic problems – inequality or the financial or environmental crisis – are too complex and intractable for any individual to tackle. Neela Bettridge and Philip Whiteley will convince you that everyone involved in corporate leadership must and can take personal responsibility. This book will set business leaders on the path toward addressing these profoundly important questions.

Diane Coyle, Director, Enlightenment Economics,
and author of *The Economics of Enough*

Bettridge and Whiteley present a compelling indictment of conventional measures used to gauge leadership performance in public and private enterprises. Stressing the illogical emphases on measures such as growth in GDP or quarterly earnings as consistent with long-term sustainability they bring substance to the much-ballyhooed catchphrase of sustainability that is more often than not part of the feel-good lexicon of corporate and governmental leaders. George Bernard Shaw aptly described the thesis of New Normal: Radical Shift when he wrote that all progress depends upon the unreasonable man. Bettridge and Whiteley dare to be unreasonable in offering a prescription for avoiding the recurring lessons of accounting scandals and asset bubbles of the twenty-first century by adoption of leadership assessments more in sync with today's dynamic global economic and political climate.

Jim Neal, contributing writer, *Newsweek*, founder of The Agema Group
and candidate for US Senate 2008

Whiteley and Bettridge have written a challenging but highly readable book. Thankfully, they go way beyond a ritualistic denunciation of 'business as usual' to offer some practical ideas about how business can change for the better. There is no doubting the urgency of the argument they make. Come with an open mind and be prepared to have your assumptions tested.

Stefan Stern, director of strategy at Edelman and Visiting Professor at
Cass Business School, UK and formerly FT management columnist

NEW NORMAL – INTRODUCTION

There are thousands of books on leadership and governance; perhaps hundreds of thousands. Why add another?

We argue that the reason is compelling, because while the library of leadership books is crowded, it does have room for an elephant. And it is this: the literature largely overlooks the fact that the most important decisions in politics and corporations are not informed by the principles of sound leadership at all. When it comes to the very biggest decisions: on economic policy, public spending, departmental or corporate restructuring, mergers and acquisitions, they are cast aside. This omission applies to the public and private sector alike.

It is worse than just benign neglect. The principles upon which the most important decisions that affect our lives are made actually undermine sound leadership and governance. They emphasise presentation over performance; the short term over the long term; targets over quality. They discourage ethical conduct and long-term stewardship, and facilitate political and financial fraud. They make organizations and economies more unstable than they could be. They seek to make environmental and employee welfare the enemy of profit. They distort our understanding of risk and of society.

The accountancy scandals of the early 2000s, the failures of risk management in banking that gave rise to the credit crisis, the high rates of failure of government projects and mergers and acquisitions, dangerous ecological degradation and volatile commodity prices, point to systemic failures and flawed thinking.

This is changing, but only slowly. In our work we come across many examples of enlightened leadership, creating strong organisations that perform across a range of measures: financial, societal and environmental. There has been impressive innovation in the past decade. Yet to achieve this, leaders often have work against the biases of the governance infrastructure in which they operate, and the attitudes that support them, in a febrile atmosphere of quarterly accounts, 24-hour news, and short tenure among many posts in commerce and government.

Through a succession of tiny steps over the past few decades, we have built up a governance infrastructure, and habits of thought, that are hopelessly ill-equipped for the challenges we face, to such an extent that they represent an obstacle.

For the twenty-first century, two massive challenges dwarf all others:

> **Governance** – how organisations and economies are run, based on an understanding of the interdependence of different constituencies, incorporating a full recognition that they are the servants of people, not the other way around. The twentieth-century model is based on a superficial understanding of the organisation: an emphasis on structure, measurement by accountancy, a short-term focus and knowledge of the workforce that is limited to the very top cadre of individuals. This demands a fundamental shift to looking at capability and understanding organisations and economies as dynamic entities.
>
> **The environment** – a proper recognition that expansion based on a tacit assumption of infinite resources is unsustainable in pure business terms, as well as environmentally. Relentless pursuit of growth with this false belief creates chronic volatility in commodity prices, and economic and political instability. The possibility of climate change is just one of many environmental constraints that all business and political leaders will have to address. Even if significant global warming does not occur, we will have to make radical improvements in our stewardship of precious resources, particularly water, arable land and commodities, as the world population grows. In the early centuries of scientific discovery and technological development, there was an understandable focus on making human beings safe from the environment. A major challenge of the coming century is to protect the environment from us. This is a seismic shift in culture and attitude that needs to occur within scientific disciplines, politics and commerce. There are some highly promising examples of this shift beginning to take place, as we shall discuss in the book.

Human beings have successfully tackled similarly momentous challenges in the past. In the nineteenth and twentieth centuries, many societies made huge progress in reducing hazards from infectious diseases, poor sanitation, illiteracy, irregular food supply, poor housing and so on. We can solve the contemporary challenges, too. But it does not help to push to the sidelines the very assets that we need to harness – skills, leadership, ingenuity, invention – and to overlook them in the biggest decisions that our organisations and governments take.

For example, why is the finance minister more high profile than the skills minister? Why is training treated as a cost and not an investment? Why is it a fight to get human capital into the annual report, when it is the source of all assets? Why do quarterly reports of profits or gross domestic product (GDP) growth dominate public discussion, ahead of more important matters such as technological innovation and leadership capability? Why is environmental concern treated as a separate category from business concerns? Why are there calls for 'labour market reform' but never for 'management reform'? What is the basis for assuming that management across the west is un-improvable, even amid copious evidence of its failures?

We will do everything, the current orthodoxy assumes, to reform economies and business sectors that have failed, except changing the beliefs, behaviours, attitudes and decision-making processes of the people who run them.

In order to meet the challenges of our day, business and political leaders have to go against the popular consensus; so in this book we shall argue that the consensus has to change. Paul Polman, Chief Executive of Unilever, made a brave announcement as he unveiled his company's sustainability strategy in November 2010. Responding to the question about the shareholder interest, he replied:

> *Unilever has been around for 100-plus years. We want to be around for several hundred more years. So if you buy into this long-term value-creation model, which is equitable, which is shared, which is sustainable, then come and invest with us. If you don't buy into this, I respect you as a human being, but don't put your money in our company.*

To those immersed in the short-termist culture that has taken hold in recent decades, this sounds like executive suicide. In the wake of the credit crisis, where many institutions lost fortunes pursuing the narrative of ever-quicker, ever-higher returns, he stands a chance. In this book, we set out to make the case that his approach makes sense for investors as well as other stakeholders. We must not waste the opportunities that this crisis creates.

CHAPTER 1

REFRAMING

On 20 April 2010, the Deepwater Horizon oil rig, owned by Transocean on behalf of BP, exploded with the loss of 11 lives. Two days later, it sank. Oil began gushing into the Gulf of Mexico, and the spill was not capped until 15 July, following some unsuccessful attempts, while permanent closure was announced on 19 September. The total leakage was estimated at nearly five million barrels. The direct cost to BP was over $3 billion; the reputational damage was incalculable.

The Deepwater Horizon disaster serves as a perfect metaphor for the conventional approach to organisational governance. We are often out of our depth, handling complex entities that can explode without warning, with tool-kits that are inadequate, where risk is incalculable and unexpected consequences far-reaching and unpredictable.

There is also paradox: an apparent emphasis on cost-cutting ended up being more expensive to the company than a more cautious approach to oil drilling and to safety. The disaster also placed a question mark over BP's strategy, as its plans for growth have depended upon extracting oil from difficult-to-access locations. The drama also illustrated the delicate interdependence of ourselves and the environment; and of different industries. Fishing and tourism in the southern USA have obviously been badly affected, and the consequences are likely to last for years. The oil industry cannot operate as though other industries do not exist; and all enterprises have to acknowledge that respect for the environment is a business as well as an ethical concern.

This tragedy came at the end of a decade punctuated by organisational and economic crises of increasing magnitude, though with recurring features. The accountancy scandals; the credit crisis; mismanagement of mergers & acquisitions (M&A). This begs some big questions. What is the nature of these events? Were they avoidable? Why did they take most of us by surprise?

If you look at the core features of these dramas, they are behavioural and international. There has been herd-like behaviour among investors, deception by executives (in the case of the accountancy scandals), decisions to minimise cost and boost quarterly figures, greed that led to risky levels of leverage and securitisation; all of these activities taking place in a global context, with limited capital controls and free trade, and deep interconnectedness of different constituencies.

Yet if you look at the information sources that we use to assess performance and risk, they are neither behavioural nor international. They are superficial, at company or national level, financial and historic.

In later chapters, we will discuss reporting methodologies and leadership approaches that better meet contemporary challenges, based on our joint experience, and numerous examples from successful organisations. There is perhaps not so much a need to develop new thinking; the thinking exists. The challenge is to convert it from the fringe to the mainstream. It is about communication.

We pretend we rely on data, but actually we buy stories. Enron was a story, securitised mortgage debt was a story, Bernie Madoff peddled a story. We know frighteningly little about the organisations that we invest in or report on. It is difficult to be fully informed on organisations; even the executives themselves cannot know everything about a large enterprise's activities and risks.

At which point, we ourselves have to observe a cautionary note. The case studies that we shall present in this book are not – indeed cannot – be based on full information. We cannot guarantee that Westpac or Marks & Spencer won't hit problems or even crises at some point in the future, but we have sought to base our reports on descriptions of the real company's activities, not just a checklist of financial indicators. In our case studies we attempt to portray some of the features of enlightened leadership; not claim that everything can be perfect.

We do not intend to produce a simplistic Good Company/Bad Company league table. Many of the corporate casualties of the past decade, such as Anglo Irish Bank and Arthur Anderson, had teams of high-integrity people delivering valuable services, but who were let down by excessive risk-taking or fraud elsewhere in the organisation. No amount of reform can offer a complete safeguard against malpractice.

The point of the cautionary tales in this chapter is to seek to learn from them; to enquire deeply into how misleading an apparently positive narrative can be. Above all, it is to highlight the common point that we systematically misread a situation owing to the dislocation referred to: the most common ways of seeking to understand, monitor and manage organisations and economies are not even in the same dimensional frame as the context in which they take place. At best they are proxy measures; at worst they are misleading or irrelevant.

Specifically, the over-reliance on quarterly financial information, and demand for a continual narrative of quarter-by-quarter 'growth', defined at company or national level, heightens risk and limits the kind of insight required to understand the behavioural dynamics that actually determine performance. Developing a broader approach to governance that seeks to understand and report on complexity and interconnectedness is not a guarantee against problems, but it is an approach that increases the sources of intelligence that can guard against error or excessive risk.

It helps if we redefine the organisation or the economy. Accountancy and formal economics have so completely captured this area that we can forget that their terms of reference are arbitrary, subjective and narrow. Within this orthodoxy, the organisation is defined as a set of assets and financial indicators; the economy appears as little more than output. If, instead, we redefine them as human communities, dependent upon the nurturing of skills and wise stewardship of finite resources, the terms of reference are transformed. The question of 'sustainability', which is core to the discussion in this book, becomes central, rather than the favoured subject matter of a few interest groups or environmental enthusiasts. This definition of sustainability covers multiple dimensions: environmental, societal and organisationally. It has, moreover, become an inescapable challenge, not an optional extra.

It has often been asserted that an approach to business that focuses on short-term maximisation of shareholder value, reducing workers to disposable human resources, and regarding natural resources as no more than a cost on the bottom line, is unethical. It is now clear that it is impractical also; bad for business as well as society and the environment.

ENRON ET AL.: JUST AN HORS D'OEUVRE

For six consecutive years, 1995–2000, the US energy giant Enron was named as *Fortune's* 'Most Innovative Company'. Everyone knows what happened subsequently, as details of the gigantic fraud began to emerge in 2001: the company went into liquidation and its leaders to prison. There has even been a play on the subject in London's West End. We do not wish here to indulge in Schadenfreude at the expense of the good people of *Fortune*; nor can we claim that we saw it coming. The point here in referring to this scandal is to make a case that the lessons have still not been learned. The context in which the key Enron executives, Kenneth Lay, Jeff Skilling and Andrew Fastow, operated encouraged this type of behaviour, and remains largely unreformed. Investors and business journalists believed the story because they wanted to, and would have reacted negatively to a more honest portrayal of company risk had it been presented to them at an earlier date.

The responses to Enron and similar cases have been to tighten financial regulation. This is understandable and necessary, but insufficient. There has been little critique of the primacy of financial reporting: judging an organisation primarily on its quarter-by-quarter profit figures. This habit creates a clear incentive for executives, many of whom have no long-term stake in the business, to boost profits figures in unsustainable ways, without a care to the long-term health or even viability of the enterprise. The *Financial Times* investigation into Enron concluded:

> *Enron bolstered profits by booking income immediately on contracts that would take up to 10 years to complete. It shifted debts into partnerships it created and in effect controlled, even though defined by auditors as off balance sheet. It used such entities to manipulate its accounts at the end of each quarter and employed financial derivatives and other complex transactions aggressively to the same end. It masked poorly performing assets with rapid deal-making.*

As an example, one of the many 'arm's-length' entities created by Enron, controlled by the corporation but effectively off balance-sheet, was LJM2 CoInvestment. In a company presentation in October 2000 it listed 24 investments since formation in December 1999. Half came in the final month of a quarter and nine in the last week of the accounting period. After the truth came to light, in 2002, the report by the special investigative committee commissioned by the Enron board said the rapid reversal of many of these deals and the fact that LJM partnerships 'made a profit on *every* transaction … call into question the legitimacy of the sale'.[1]

The chief measure that companies have employed over the past few decades to guard against executives acting against the interest of the company and shareholders is based on something called 'agency theory', which will be discussed in more detail in Chapter 3. Proponents of agency theory recommend that executives build up significant stockholdings in the company. In the case of Enron, this simply further encouraged them to shore up the stock price by any means available, and then offload their personal holdings before the bad news hit the wires.

The policeman that the architects of the contemporary governance structure devised, agency theory, ended up as complicit in the crime. Despite this, there has been little fundamental inquiry into the flawed nature of this theory and the damage it has wrought; and inadequate initiatives at ideological renewal. The formulaic and superficial stipulations of successive codes of conduct in governance miss the point. They consider structures of committees; create a bogus, and actually unlawful, concept of 'independent' board directors; and ignore behavioural dynamics altogether. Again, we shall discuss this further in Chapter 3.

There is an irony: the more that individuals insist that they follow 'hard' financial data rather than a qualitative narrative, the more susceptible they become to a misleading story. The more they deny their emotions, the more prone they are to irrational exuberance.

---

1   Enron: Virtual company, virtual profits, *Financial Times* special report, 3 February 2002.

The scandal at Enron, which occurred at a time of similar frauds at WorldCom, Global Crossing, Tyco and others, had the following characteristics: excessive focus on short-term financial growth; reliance on superficial economic indicators; an unsustainable bubble in asset prices; a sudden collapse in price, with a few insiders reaping huge rewards while many investors lose billions of dollars.

What if such a pattern were to repeat itself, not at a corporate level, but across entire economies? Step forward the credit crisis. In the multi-course feast of gluttony, waste, ruin and stupidity in the first decade of the twenty-first century, Enron et al. were just the hors d'oeuvres.

COLLATORISED DEBT OBLIGATIONS, HOUSING BUBBLES AND ECONOMIC 'GROWTH'

A marked feature of Enron was its aggressive use of financial engineering, especially derivatives to bring forward profit, or at least the appearance of profit, and reliance upon optimistic forecasting as justification for the reported results. As the fraudulent use of such activities became apparent, a similar derivative was becoming popular in the banking industry. Collatorised Debt Obligations (CDOs) were a form securitising mortgage debt. The intention was to spread risk among lower-grade debts, but the practice soon became divorced from the underlying assets, and excessive optimism took over, sending the trading value of such derivatives higher, even though the traders had no way of knowing the viability of the debtors involved. Meanwhile, aggressive sub-prime lending in many nations: especially the USA, Spain, Ireland and the UK, sent house prices higher and increased the hidden risk within CDO trading. In Spain and Ireland in particular, property companies piled in, building excessively on the strength of the upward march of real estate prices. It was a classic 'bubble', but cheered on by the financial pages, finance ministers and the banks.

Economic theory exacerbated the problem in CDO trading. Excessive reliance on financial data has tempted economists and investment banks down some dangerous paths. As Nassim Nicholas Taleb observed in *Black Swan*,[2] economic orthodoxy has clung to the pretence that economics observes Newtonian, predictable properties. The generation of so much data meant that advanced calculus could be used to 'plot' the behaviour of asset prices as a means of assessing risk. The fact that such plotting has no relation to real life has never deterred such economists. It is unlikely that calculus has a valid role at all in economics, because there are no constants. In the time it takes to complete the calculation, the operating assumptions used to inform it have altered, rendering it useless.

---

2   Taleb, Nassim Nicholas, *The Black Swan: The Impact of the Highly Improbable*, Random House, 2007.

Taleb anticipated the crisis in 2007, just before it hit:

> *The giant firm JP Morgan put the entire world at risk by introducing, in the 1990s, RiskMetrics, a phony method aiming at managing people's risks ... A related method called 'Value at Risk', which relies on the quantitative measurement of risk, has been spreading. Likewise, the government-sponsored institution Fanny Mae, when I look at their risks, seems to be sitting on a barrel of dynamite, vulnerable to the slightest hiccup. But not to worry: their large staff of scientists deemed these events 'unlikely'.*

The dynamite did indeed explode just a few months later. Here is a paradox: an individual who eschews prediction was more correct in his anticipation of events than those who pretended you could predict with accuracy.

At a political level, it is alarming that the same superficial indicators that have proved so misleading and inadequate at corporate level should also be applied at national level, where the complexity is even greater and the stakes even higher.

The definition of recession as two quarters of successive negative growth creates a huge incentive for politicians to maintain the illusion of 'growth', especially in the run-up to an election, even if this is in unsustainable ways. News media feed into this illusion, putting fierce pressure on politicians to come up with 'growth' by any means. By this measure, reckless state borrowing and debt-fuelled consumption binges look as positive as growth based on the development of an innovative engineering sector.

The behavioural pattern is identical to that of CEOs bolstering short-term profits figures. To take one example, Ireland was dubbed the 'Celtic Tiger' because of continuous GDP growth, and insufficient attention was paid to the levels of risk. House price rises are assumed to be beneficial to an economy even when they soar far above a reasonable level of affordability for the real economy. In the mid-2000s in Ireland, leading economist Morgan Kelly of University College Dublin began warning of dangerous levels of debt, particularly excessive exposure of banks to the construction sector. Yet rather than take heed, the then Taioseach (prime minister) Bertie Ahern rounded on him angrily in an outburst in which he wondered if Professor Kelly should kill himself. Mr Ahern's actual words said that the act of people such as Professor Kelly 'sitting on the sidelines and the fence, cribbing and moaning is a lost opportunity'. He added: 'In fact, I don't know how people who engage in that don't commit suicide'. He later apologised for the suicide reference, but not for the complacency on economic stewardship.[3]

---

3   Support groups criticise Ahern over 'appalling and offensive' comments, *Irish Independent*, 5 July 2007. Available at: http://www.independent.ie/national-news/support-groups-criticise-ahern-over-appalling-and-offensive-comments-955848.html [accessed 2 August 2012].

Ireland's government ministers, like many others around the world, did not want the narrative of 'growth' interrupted by the discordant tones of reality.

We cannot expect any prime minister to completely understand all sources of risk in an economy and guard against them. The point here is a different one: it is about learning to constrain the biases that encourage irrational exuberance. If 'growth' is arbitrarily prioritised ahead of sustainability, then asset price inflation is more likely to occur, and less likely to be curbed before it reaches dangerous levels. We can start to recognise house price inflation as a potential source of instability, rather than effortless wealth accumulation. If we can alter our mindsets and lexicon away from growth towards sustainability, defined broadly, this can help our economic stewardship, as well as our planet.

So while some technical lessons are being learned at the level of the banks since the credit crisis broke, and hopefully products such as CDOs-squared will never again be let loose on the economy, there has been no deeper learning. Such toxic products are an inevitable by-product of the deeply flawed way in which economics and organisational management are dangerously biased towards growth, or typically the appearance of growth, rather than sustainability.

In the case of the banking sector, this has been made worse by exponential growth in bonuses awarded to those who traded in such products. And the adoption of accountancy profit, rather than economic profit, exacerbated the problems. Peter Christie, a former head of compensation at Midland Montagu and later a reward adviser at the Hay Group, argues that economic profit, which accounts for underwriting costs, would be a much wiser basis for awarding bonuses than a simple year-end bottom line figure, which incentivised risky trading. He wrote in 2008:

> With loans, derivatives and under-writing, the ways in which they are structured do not fall neatly into the 12-monthly accounting period. They create a tail of liability for the organisation. The liability may be securitised and traded off, but that tail liability does not disappear – it stays in the system, and it may increase. Over the past ten years there has been growth in the value of bonuses, but the design of the bonuses has not changed to reflect the tail of liabilities.[4]

MERGERS & ACQUISITIONS

An area with an even longer history of misallocation of capital and weak governance than corporate accounting fraud or housing bubbles can be seen in

---

4   Latest Ideas in Reward, by Peter Christie. Chapter in Whiteley, Philip, ed., *Strategic Risk & Reward*, Thomson Reuters, 2008.

M&A activity. It is well established that most mergers fail; we even know why. Yet the failed patterns of behaviour keep getting repeated. This is because the flawed underlying beliefs go unchecked and unreformed. The core problem is the same as that encountered with Enron and CDOs: the pretence that financial indicators plot reality, and can be used for projections into the future. Hence, executives anticipate 'economies of scale' and 'synergies' based on merging two sets of financial data, forgetting that a merger actually consists of people, who behave in unpredictable ways. As with the accounting scandals, the cult of quarterly reporting, and a feverish desire for a narrative of ever-upward earnings, helps to fuel the empire-building.

When the almost inevitable crisis hits, executives blame 'culture clashes' – precisely the dimension that they studiously ignore when plotting the union. The real mystery is why the buy-side has kept getting suckered, but there are promising indications that they are beginning to wise up, as shall be discussed further in Chapter 4. An argument that one can come across is that merger failure is part of the 'creative destruction' of capitalism. This is a lazy, catch-all alibi for some examples of quite gratuitous corporate damage. Recent examples include Time Warner-AOL, Daimler-Chrysler, Royal Bank of Scotland-ABN and Citibank-Travelers.

In one of the most recent mega-mergers, Kraft-Cadbury, there was little evidence that lessons have been learned from past mistakes, though of course it is possible that Kraft possesses sufficient management capability to see it through. In early 2010, Irene Rosenfeld and the Kraft board claimed to have identified $675 million of cost savings by merging the two confectionary giants. This claim is highly questionable, as it appears to rest on projections based on past trends of two separate companies. The main source of cost, and of efficiency, and of value, is human performance, and this is seriously affected by a merger, which invariably has unexpected side-effects. In the case of Kraft-Cadbury, one example was the loss of key senior executives, including Phil Rumbol, the marketing executive who had overseen the highly valuable 'gorilla' advertising campaign. Following one such departure, Chris Bones, a former Cadbury HR manager who became a professor at Manchester Business School, told Bloomberg News: 'Given Cadbury were seen as having the stronger confectionery management team, the loss of another senior former Cadbury manager must increase concerns among Kraft shareholders'.

In the absence of advanced human capital analytics, it is impossible to gauge the impact of such losses from the management team. What is certain is that the systemic failure to include such risk analysis in merger due diligence is a serious weakness. We cannot be certain that such defections will seriously weaken Kraft-Cadbury, but the Kraft executives cannot be certain that they won't, and they appear unprepared.

Numerous studies over the past few decades have illustrated the low likelihood of complex mergers to be effective. Those mostly likely to succeed are where there is a clear takeover, typically of a smaller specialist firm by a much larger company; a good cultural match and an emphasis upon acquisition of skills or expertise, rather than spurious projections of 'synergy' or economies of scale.

One analysis of more than 200 major European M&As over a three-year period by the Hay Group consultancy in 2007 found that senior business leaders regarded just 9 per cent of mergers as having been 'completely successful' in achieving their stated objectives. 'The M&A feeding frenzy over the last year has been fuelled not only by cheap debt and the rise of private equity, but also by companies' strategic focus on consolidation', according to report author David Derain, European M&A director at Hay. 'However, the enormous amounts invested in M&A are not delivering their promised value'. He added:

> Business leaders must recognise that the value of today's companies is primarily in ... the strategic, people and cultural factors that don't show up on a balance sheet. Culture is not an HR issue – it is a business issue. Business culture represents a class of assets which must be protected and properly aligned during the integration process if a merger is to succeed.[5]

These findings were the same as those eight years earlier in a KPMG study on merger failure and success, 'Unlocking Shareholder Value'. This found that most mergers failed, and that there was a significantly higher chance of success in examples where close attention was paid to the composition of the management team, communications and cultural issues.[6]

FAILED GOVERNMENTAL PROJECTS

Every year, in many jurisdictions, there are newspaper headlines about millions of euros/pounds/dollars lost through wasteful public sector projects. This includes the many cases where private sector suppliers are used. One would think that waste and mismanagement were almost inevitable.

Yet there is huge difference between the best and the worst-run projects. Good news does not make a headline. No ambitious reporter will run to his or her news editor, breathlessly exclaiming: 'The contract to build that railway terminus came in on schedule and under budget!'

As with large mergers, the difference lies in the calibre of project management. Yet, in another similarity with the corporate world, relatively little attention is paid to this crucial dimension, prior to execution, or sometimes even afterwards. The sales

---

5   Dangerous Liaisons: Mergers & Acquisitions – The Integration Game, Hay Group report, March 2007. See www.haygroup.com
6   Unlocking Shareholder Value: The Keys to Success, KPMG paper, 1999.

pitch for an IT or outsourcing programme in the public sector bears a strong family resemblance to the prospectus for a merger: we are promised economies of scale, access to new technology and new skills, and projections of cost savings. The test lies in the execution but, as with mergers, there is sometimes scant assessment of, or planning for, the management capability necessary to reach these ambitious aims.

The poor image of public sector management leads to an understandable emphasis on increasing the level of outsourcing. This is a superficial response, for two reasons. First of all, levels of expertise are not automatically superior in the private sector. Secondly, the very act of negotiating and handling an outsourcing arrangement is itself a major managerial challenge, and one that is often underestimated. The public sector cannot contract out its responsibilities.

In the UK in April 2011, the former head of IT for the Government, Ian Watmore, said that high-profile technology fiascos in the past had been caused by overambition and poor project management, not by defects in the technology. He told a House of Commons committee that ministers simply ordered IT as an 'after thought … or worse, there were people thinking they needed to have a piece of technology to make their policy sound sexy'. The 'so-called IT disasters' of recent years were not really technical glitches, but the product of 'overambitious projects' that were expected to deliver complex changes at a national level in a straightforward way; 'the so-called "Big Bang" implementation'.[7]

There is a tendency in much political discourse to regard all public sector initiatives as being an economic stimulus. And, of course, they all add to GDP figures, even when dependent upon borrowing. When there is waste, however, there is an opportunity cost. Money that could be spent on true investment in human capital goes on fattened margins for suppliers with a cosy relationship with ministers; highly qualified individuals may be working in quangos of doubtful merit, rather than helping the productive economy; taxation on hard-working individuals and businesses is increased. The folly of regarding debt as progressive or a stimulus will be discussed further in Chapter 6.

THE BINARY DELUSION

All of the recent crises and problems listed above are exacerbated by a cognitive bias in human discussions, particularly in politics and the media, to reduce complex matters to either/or choices. We call this 'the binary delusion'. It is extremely difficult to discuss the subject of governance and economics when there is such marked pressure to squeeze the debate into a simplified choice between two orthodoxies – and extremely frustrating when you consider them both to be inadequate or false.

---

7   Whitehall IT chief Ian Watmore attacks Labour's record, BBC online, 30 March 2011.

In economic theory, especially, some 'opposing' ideas often resemble one another more than they differ.

Neo-liberal versus Keynesian

Following the credit crisis, and the consequent surge in sovereign debt as western governments took on the liabilities of the failed banking system, debate has raged between economists on ways out of the crisis. The dominant arguments come from the traditional camps. Neo-liberals favour cutting public spending sharply, releasing the private sector which, they argue, becomes 'crowded out' by high government borrowing and spending. Keynesians argue that borrowing is legitimate to sustain demand through difficult economic conditions, that cutting too sharply risks a double-dip recession. Continued borrowing and spending is a 'fiscal stimulus'.

From neither side is there so much as a whisper on what public sector funds might actually be spent. Nor is there proper concern for how value for money for any investment, public or private, can be assessed.

The entire lexicon of economics is based on a mechanistic metaphor that an economy is just gigantic plumbing, with money like flowing water: aggregate demand, crowding out, fiscal stimulus, and so on. For example, the 'crowding out' agenda is based on the assumption that public spending is often wasted. Now, it probably is, but so is much private investment, such as wasteful or poorly planned mergers, as discussed.

In the conventional economic theories that guide the policies we experience, the people who actually create the wealth do not even feature. As Gordon Pearson notes in his masterful book *The Rise and Fall of Management*:

> While variations have occurred at different times, economic theories, from Marx to Keynes and Friedman, share both a common root in Adam Smith and a more or less complete incomprehension of business enterprise and its management.[8]

In terms of monitoring economic developments, the main indicator remains the embarrassingly crude 'money in, money out' double-entry book-keeping technique, developed by Luca Pacioli in the 1490s. This still forms the basis of the quarterly report, together with the similarly crude GDP growth indicator for a national economy, but with the unfortunate adaptation that booked profit or borrowed growth is allowed to be registered, meaning that the headline figures are often fictional as well as mono-dimensional.

---

8   Pearson, Gordon, *The Rise and Fall of Management*, Gower Publishing, 2012.

We are dealing with a twenty-first century inbox of acute environmental pressure; complex, international organisations, depending on high levels of skill and technological awareness. Yet our ways of understanding these dynamics rest on flawed eighteenth to twentieth-century economic thinking, and our main means of measurement and communication is an unreformed fifteenth-century technique. It is like trying to guide a rocket to the moon using the navigational instruments of Christopher Colombus.

Global Warmism versus Climate Scepticism

Another energy-wasting distraction is the increasingly bitter partisan argument between proponents and detractors from the principal global warming theories. For all their mutual hatred, the participants share the common point that proving, or disproving, global warming is the only ecological or scientific challenge of our day worthy of serious discussion. Perspective, as well as truth, was an early casualty of this ideological war.

A more rounded viewpoint is to take seriously the actual and potential hazards of CO_2 emissions, but as one challenge among a daunting agenda of environmental pressures, which should also include stewardship of water, arable land and commodities.

The errors and exaggerations of some climate change campaigners have to be corrected. They have spawned an entire publishing industry of sceptics. Many of these sceptics make valid points about skewed research, but they are straining at gnats while swallowing camels. Even if all the sceptics' claims turn out to be true on the narrow issue of warming, then what? Will it still be safe to continue poisoning the very air that we breathe by increasing still further the proportion that is CO_2? Would we do this to the water that we drink? Will it still be sustainable to pretend that finite resources are infinite?

SUSTAINABILITY AS A MEGATREND

The common problem to the false choices summarised above is that they frame the problems that face us in a way that arbitrarily ignores some of the most important questions. The result is euphemism and evasion, and delayed reaction to crisis.

Below the newspaper and online headlines, however, there is leadership. We see it in the venture capitalists backing new technologies to conquer environmental ills, and in the far-sighted governance of corporations that see sustainability as the new normal, rather than a chapter in the corporate social responsibility report. Indeed, it is possible to take an optimistic view and assert that sustainability is the new megatrend. This is the conclusion of David A. Lubin and Daniel C. Esty, writing in the *Harvard Business Review* in May 2010. They cite examples of long-established corporations making serious moves towards sustainable practices across the board, such as Coca Cola, IBM and Wal-Mart. A philosophy that, a decade ago, might have been confined to some pioneering companies like Whole Foods and Ben & Jerry's, is reaching the mainstream.

The authors liken it to similar shifts towards total quality and automation in the 1980s and 1990s:

> *Just as the quality and IT megatrends ushered in new skill sets and fresh perspectives, the sustainability megatrend will require firms to update traditional business tools – business-case analysis, trend spotting, scenario planning, risk modelling, and even cost accounting – to encompass the specialised requirements of environmental sustainability.*[9]

IN SUMMARY

The attitudes and structures of political and organisational management have caused an excessive focus on short-term results, and a superficial understanding of costs and risks, making systemic crises highly likely and vast in scope. Carrying on with the model that hit crisis in the period 2000–2010 is not a viable option. As the commercial and ethical achievements of institutions embracing the new normal become more well known, the onus is inverted. Instead of executives asking, 'Can we afford to be dedicated to sustainability?' the question becomes, 'Can we afford not to?' In the rest of this book, we shall disseminate some ideas and practical examples that illustrate how the challenge is being met.

---

9   Lubin, David A. and Esty, Daniel C., The Sustainability Imperative, *Harvard Business Review*, May 2010.

CHAPTER 2

A MULTI-POLAR WORLD AND A FINITE ONE

We are living in an age of momentous change. As we write, North Africa and the Middle East are undergoing a wave of revolutions, similar to those of the former Communist bloc in 1989. Just as had occurred a generation earlier in eastern Europe, when unrepresentative oligarchical elites were forced from power, the process varies from comparatively peaceful to attritional and bloody.

China has just become the world's second largest economy, and looks destined to become its biggest. The Wikileaks revelations of diplomatic secrets include a glimpse of how China has already begun using its status as the biggest creditor to an indebted US to gain diplomatic leverage. In February 2011, the leaked report stated that 'escalating Chinese pressure prompted a procession of soothing visits from the US Treasury Department. In one striking instance, a top Chinese money manager directly asked US Treasury Secretary Timothy Geithner for a favour'. The favour in question had come in June 2009 when the head of China's principal sovereign wealth fund met with Geithner and requested that he 'lean on' regulators at the US Federal Reserve to speed up the approval of its $1.2 billion investment in Morgan Stanley. The cables do not specify whether Geithner took any action, but China's deal to buy Morgan Stanley shares was announced the following day[1] Such influence over Washington would have been unthinkable even a decade earlier.

China is increasingly the dominant external power in Africa, some regions of which have the potential to become rising economic powers. According to a report by the South Africa-based Standard Bank, China is Africa's largest trading partner; trade between the two has doubled every three years for the past 15 years. Chinese investment in the continent is expected to reach $50 billion by 2015.[2] The extent to which China's interest is colonial in nature, based on export of raw materials, or whether it is genuine mutual interest of equal trading partners, is the subject of considerable debate. There are significant advantages for Chinese manufacturers with access to commodities, but many of the infrastructure projects that Chinese

---

1   Special report: China flexed its muscles using US Treasuries, Reuters, 17 February 2011.

2   China will increase investment in Africa, says Standard Bank, *Finance Asia*, 29 March 2011.

capital has helped develop are likely to be of lasting benefit to the continent, according to a World Bank report.[3] Brazil and India are enjoying similar economic development to that of China. Education standards in many emerging economies are now ahead of many industrialised nations. The age of western domination appears to be coming to an end.

These are the kind of developments that make the news headlines. Underneath the geo-politics, ordinary 'real' trade continues to chug along nicely, with growing business development and rising living standards in the emerging economies. Many enterprises in the 'old' economies, for example German manufacturers, are also thriving. Yet the increasing number of middle class consumers and rising global population are already beginning to hit against the most formidable barrier to traditional industrial-style economic growth: the finite nature of the earth's resources.

This, then, is the modern world: it is no longer run by the west – which faces a colossal debt burden; there are many millions of people being lifted out of poverty as emerging economies develop, yet this takes place in a world of huge inequalities, confronting a perfect ecological storm.

This book cannot offer easy answers to such formidable problems. Its purpose is rather different: it is to describe how businesses and leaders can play a positive role. Most of the critiques of recent economic developments and ideologies lump all corporations together and treat a vaguely defined 'globalisation' as the enemy. This is crude and unhelpful; the sort of anti-business agenda that borders on misanthropy. A business is neither good nor bad, inherently. Profits may be made in exploitative or in enlightened ways, and the latter tend to be features of the more resilient and successful firms. In addition, a profit-making business is as likely as a non-profit organisation to have a neutral or positive effect on the environment. Global trading might increase inequalities, or decrease them. The first distinction to make, then, is between 'good' and 'bad' globalisation.

GOOD GLOBALISATION, BAD GLOBALISATION

One feature that appears to accompany globalisation of the economy is extreme, and apparently rising, economic inequality. It is important, however, to identify the causes of this, to identify counter-currents, and to identify matters that are wrongly held to be a cause of inequality. We argue that the rising inequalities are primarily a result of excess credit and celebrity economics, not the way in which the vast bulk of profit-making businesses work. It is essential to understand the distinction between

---

3   Building Bridges: China's Growing Role as Infrastructure Financier for Sub-Saharan Africa, Vivien Foster, William Butterfield, Chuan Chen and Nataliya Pushak, World Bank Policy Paper, July 2008.

these three features of the global, hi-tech, environmentally threatened economy. The way in which excess credit and globalised media operate is to increase inequalities, to an extreme degree in many contexts. But an increasing need for high skills, high levels of service and engagement of customers and staff in many parts of the 'real' economy are favoured by reduced inequalities. To give some examples, international teams developing exciting new smart phones (very popular with all those anti-capitalist protestors, as it happens) we would describe as 'good globalisation'; while using hot money to cash in on an unsustainable credit boom in securitised mortgage trading or government bonds is 'bad globalisation'.

The potential for harnessing the natural tendency towards reduced inequality in the production of socially valuable goods and services is, however, hampered by the slowness of business leaders and trade unions to recognise the potential. Most do not yet possess the ideology or the vocabulary to describe and encourage the economics of interdependence; for example by not adopting human capital analysis which, where used, shows the huge business returns of high levels of employee engagement and promising careers for staff. Some of the most commercially successful and resilient companies have maintained or reduced differential incomes between executives and the most junior staff, and some are highlighted in this book.

RISING INEQUALITY: EXCESS CREDIT AND THE FAME GAME

It is our contention that extreme inequalities do not flow from globalised trade, but are derived more from two quite different phenomena: excess credit and the economics of celebrity status. One study indicated that, between 1989 and 2006 in the USA, the number of people earning more than $2 million a year doubled, after accounting for inflation. With the exception of CEOs of technology start-ups, nearly all the remaining professions to see huge increases in earnings were associated with finance or the industries that feed of it such as commercial law and real estate; or were sports stars or entertainment celebrities.[4]

Excess Credit

Ease of creating debt gives too much power to the banks and to careerist politicians. It is a way of printing money and passing on serious financial problems to future generations, that is quite scandalous when one analyses the actual dynamics. It can be fraudulent in effect, but probably most of the participants are guilty of short-termism, opportunism and ignorance, rather than calculated deception. Some of the most unfair phenomena concern excessive levels of borrowing, either private or government and very often both, in a currency that is effectively overvalued for

---

4   Study of US Government data by Edward Wolff, New York University, quoted in Lure of Great Wealth Affects Career Choices, *New York Times*, 27 November 2006.

the productive economy that bears the future cost. This has certainly been the case in Argentina and Greece, but is becoming a feature for much of western Europe and even the USA itself. This has distorted politics to such a degree that the distinction between 'left' and 'right' is essentially meaningless in many contexts, as will be discussed further in Chapter 6.

Where credit is easily obtainable, and powerful figures have freedom to create it, the winners are: the banks, especially the investment banks who gain transaction fees simply for organising bond issues, and so on; short-termist politicians, who are often writing their self-satisfied memoirs by the time their unsustainable boom has turned to bust and they have passed the blame on to the succeeding administration; property and other speculators who by luck or judgement cash in near the top of investment bubbles. The losers are just about everyone else, but with the complication that some of us appear to be benefiting from rising property values or higher public spending in the short term. The scale of the winning and losing has grown exponentially with the deregulation of global finance.

Even some figures from the conservative worlds of fund management and economic policy are beginning to question the policy of free-flowing capital and easy lending, and are calling for stricter controls, especially for vulnerable mid-income and poorer countries.

Revulsion against the politics of excessive credit-creation can come from fiscal conservatives and radical 'green' economists, who make similar points. Ron Paul, a Republican US senator, is a long-standing critic of 'fiat' currency systems – that is, currency that is not convertible to a precious metal or other commodity, and whose value is based on the issuing authority's guarantee to pay the stated amount. 'Fiat' is Latin for 'let it be done'.

Mr Paul warned in 2003 that a fiat currency gives too much power to the banks and to elected politicians – of left and right – as they can gain short-term benefits from printing money. But he added: 'We all deal with the consequences of our fiat money system, however. Every dollar created dilutes the value of existing dollars in circulation. Those individuals who worked hard, paid their taxes, and saved some money for a rainy day are hit the hardest. Their dollars depreciate in value while earning interest that is kept artificially low by the Federal Reserve easy-credit policy. The poor and those dependent on fixed incomes can't keep up with the rising cost of living'.[5]

Paper 'fiat' currencies have a long record of association with sudden collapses in value and hyper-inflation, especially when governments face huge debts. The reason

---

5   Fiat paper money, article by Congressman Ron Paul, September 2003. Available at: http://www.lewrockwell.com/paul/paul125.html [accessed 28 October 2012].

that collapses are sudden is that the value of the circulating paper is maintained only by trust; so once trust starts to go, people start to fear that their savings are going to become worthless, and there is a rush for the exit – it is a large-scale version of a bank run. Examples are pre-revolutionary France, the Weimar Republic in Germany and the Argentine currency and inflation crises of the past 25 years. Given that all major currencies are now fiat currencies, and that aggregate sovereign debt is both huge and rising, the implications are disquieting.

Green economists make a similar criticism of the modern system of money. Author James Robertson argues that making the simple creation of credit profitable has encouraged dangerous speculation in land and property. These have had huge distorting effects in recent years, especially in small economies like Iceland and Ireland. Money creation should be a non-profit making and under more direct democratic control, geared towards meeting social and environmental needs. Writing in *Yes!* Magazine in 2009, he argued: 'The system now in place encourages or compels us all to get and spend money in ways that work against the planet, against other people, and against ourselves'.[6]

In the aftermath of the credit crisis, one of the imperatives of elected politicians, both through quantitative easing measures and pressure put on the banks, has been to 'get the banks lending again', even though excessive lending had been the primary cause of the crisis. We would argue that there is an historic need to drastically scale back the supply of credit, and eliminate or reduce its profit-making potential, so that money becomes no more than the purpose of exchange of real goods and services. Excessive credit supply has created multiple and extreme forms of inequality: between investment banks and the real economy; between the powerful political/ banking elite and salaried staff throughout the economy; between older property owners and future generations.

One aspect to this discussion is that the critique is shared by fiscal conservatives and radical greens. We will discuss further the limitations of the 'left/right' way of considering political decisions in Chapter 6.

Celebrity Economics

Rewards in show business and sport have rocketed in the past 20 years, with the globalisation of marketing and the growth of different communications and entertainment media. The principle is: to those that have, shall be given, and audiences with purchasing power have grown considerably in size. Television chat show hosts only want award winners and gold medallists on their show. Book deals, and presenting of TV documentaries, are more likely to be awarded to a celebrity than

---

6   Robertson, James, Money from nothing: Supplying money should be a public service, not a cash cow for the banks, *Yes!* Magazine, July 2009.

to a professional author or journalist compared with a few decades ago. A tendency within news media to go big on a smaller number of stories also accentuates the inequalities between the individuals profiled in stories and features and those who are not.

The rise of sponsorship opportunities, and opening up of merchandising to a global audience, has caused the earnings potentials of the top sports stars to rise exponentially. Just a few decades ago, even top international sports stars earned little more than a reasonable salary from their active years, and typically had to find another career or start a business after retirement from competition. There are no such financial anxieties for the most famous sports-people today. In 2009, the golfer Tiger Woods became the first billionaire sportsman.

REDUCED INEQUALITY: HIGH-SKILL, HIGH-NETWORKED BUSINESSES

Until the 1980s and 1990s, the vast bulk of the value of most businesses lay in acquired assets that were under the control of the most senior executives. Raw materials were easily available, at least for the militarily and politically dominant powers, skill requirements were lower. With a mining or oil exploration company, the asset lay mostly in the ground. With a traditional manufacturing operation based on a Fordist production line, the assets lay in the equipment and distribution channels; by contrast skill levels and wages were low on the production line, and workers were easy to replace unless unemployment fell to very low levels. With harder-to-reach commodities; greater consumer choice and customisation, and greater demand for high levels of service and technologically rich functions, some of the traditional assets have become commoditised, so competitive advantage comes from the levels of service that the teams that comprise the organisation can deliver for customers. This requires very high levels of engagement and teamwork, and decent returns for everyone within the organisation.

A report in 2006 by Accenture indicated that the proportion of a company's value held in human capital had increased from around 20 per cent to 70 per cent in the previous three decades, among companies in the S&P 500.[7]

It is common to talk loosely about the value of a brand, and 'brand equity' as though it were a discrete or tradable entity. In the real world, a brand is no more or less than the combined skills, know-how and service of the people who make up the organisation. This extends beyond design and innovation to supply chains, retail

---

7   *The Talent Powered Organization: Strategies for Globalization, Talent Management and High Performance*, Peter Cheese, Robert J. Thomas and Elizabeth Craig, Accenture with Kogan Page, 2007.

staff and so on. Customers will stop buying a certain brand of smart-phone if it breaks easily, or there is a long waiting time for handsets, or if the apps do not download properly. Everything comes down to human commitment and skills.

One problem that hampers wider recognition of this development is the persistence of the misnomer 'intangible' to describe human skills. This derives from the practices of accountancy and company law, which refers to tangible assets as those that can be owned by the legal entity that is the company and priced on a balance sheet. However, the ultimate underlying value of all companies is the people who comprise it. It is people who create assets, not the other way around.

One of our main purposes in writing this book is to highlight the extent to which in the non-financial economy there are huge equalising tendencies. This is a development largely ignored by the business community and trade union movement alike. Both assume that recent widening of differentials between executives and the lowest-ranked workers is in the commercial interest. It is true that they have increased. The differential in big western companies can be 400 times, and is getting worse. The top pay of FTSE 100 bosses has jumped from 124 times the minimum wage to 202 times. But where is the evidence that this helps business performance? As far as we are aware, having followed the matter for the past decade and more, there is none. Moreover, there are indications that the evidence highlighting the importance of employee engagement and good rewards for 'ordinary' staff has been systematically overlooked. This is an historic failure of leadership.

Everyone who has used a call centre will know that the experience indicates that they are still modelled more on the example of Charles Dickens' Ebenezer Scrooge than the evidence of a high-performance workplace. The worker is seen as a cost; the performance is judged by transactional measures that bear no direct relation to service, and organisations cheerily pass direct costs on to the customer without stopping to think of the potential for lost business. Every time you are held waiting by an automated phone system, or are put through to an individual who lacks the training and product knowledge to help with your query, the company endures a significant opportunity cost that it does not bother to take into account.

This, of course, does not prove that greater equality always leads to better performance. One of the many myths one encounters in organisational and management theory is the notion that there is a single feature or simplistic formula for success. There is not. Organisations are behavioural, and human behaviour is complex. What it does indicate is that the lazy assumptions of recent decades are at best inaccurate and may be wildly wrong. According to the orthodox views of neo-liberalism and Marxism, which still dominate popular prejudices in the boardroom and on the picket line, enterprises such as Mondragon, Whole Foods, Nationwide Building Society, Semler, Google, WL Gore & Associates ought to be commercial failures. The fact that these organisations are not only successful, but exceptionally successful and resilient, tells us that something is fundamentally wrong about the dominant economic and political philosophies that still hold too much sway. The economic benefits of cooperation and equality of status are beginning to be seen, not in experimental communes, but in some of the most successful corporations in the world.

Economies need to be reorientated away from speculation, government borrowing and short-term growth, towards real human needs and sustainability. This does not compromise the profit motive, or the understandable desire for people to have a good quality of life.

RISING INEQUALITY IS NOT INEVITABLE – OR IN THE BUSINESS INTEREST

It is important to make the distinction between these three areas: excess credit creation, the celebrity phenomenon and the high-skill, networked business. The first two tend towards greater inequality; the last towards lesser inequality – at least, where the business leaders recognise the hidden potential of interdependence.

At the moment, there is huge pressure to reduce inequalities through high levels of public spending. Where this involves borrowing, however, it actually worsens inequalities by passing more power and rent-seeking opportunities to the banking industry and creating a debt for younger and future generations, including those on low incomes. The politics of excess credit do not pass the green test either, as they encourage current consumption over sustainability. They use economic indicators that record all public expenditure as being an economic stimulus and regarded as a social good, even if it is spent in ecologically unsustainable ways, or wasted on unproductive quangos. So in the west, in particular, there is a vicious circle in operation. The dominant strategy being deployed to lessen inequality actually increases it, in at least some dimensions, and particularly between generations. One implication is to rethink our political assumptions and terms of reference, as we shall discuss further in Chapter 6.

ONE WORLD

Much of the environmental debate in recent years has been expended on attempting to prove or disprove various theories around the global warming effect of CO_2 emissions. This is an important debate, but it is far from being the only environmental concern, and may not even prove to be the most important. The terms of reference for the debate are revealing: the onus is put on anti-carbon emission campaigners to prove that CO_2 emissions are leading to dangerous climate change. The tacit assumption is that it is reasonable to revert to twentieth-century style petro-fuelled economic growth if the case cannot be made, even as the emerging economies become industrialised and world population grows. The climate sceptics sometimes make valid points, but they are missing the bigger picture. The purpose of this section is to address the broader scenario: to set out in the boldest terms possible some of the environmental pressures that are building, and to point out that everyone has to confront these and amend policies accordingly – not just political leaders, but business leaders, educationalists, trade unionists, agriculturalists, government departments and so on.

Our business models – the accountancy methods we use, company-reporting procedures and assumptions around governance – are essentially unchanged since the pioneering English and Dutch companies of the seventeenth century. They are desperately in need of updating from this late-Mediaeval period. Their weaknesses were evident, for example, in the corporate collapses of the past decade, as we discussed in Chapter 1. They only concern themselves with financial accounting and ownership of inanimate resources. They date from a period prior to heavy industry, in which the naval powers of Europe seized control of much of the world's territory through force. Access to such cheap natural resources helped to fuel the industrialisation of northern and western Europe, and subsequently North America and Japan. Subsequent wars for independence represented the natural desire for the peoples of Asia, Africa and South America to regain control over their land and resources, though often weak governance and corruption meant that only the elite in those regions benefited. Throughout all these struggles, however, it was taken for granted that the supply of natural resources: land, water, fuels, metals, timber, fisheries and so on, were to all intents and purposes infinite for meeting human needs. That assumption no longer holds.

Water

The United Nations has stated that as many as 2.7 billion people could face severe water shortages by 2025 if current consumption levels continue and as the world population rises from six billion to a possible nine billion by 2050. As a *National Geographic* feature on the subject observed:

> *The amount of fresh water on Earth is not increasing. Nearly 97 percent of the planet's water is salt water in seas and oceans. Close to 2 percent of Earth's water is frozen in polar ice sheets and glaciers, and a fraction of 1 percent is available for drinking, irrigation, and industrial use.*[8]

---

8   Water pressure, Fen Montaigne, from National Geographic republished online. Available at: http://environment.nationalgeographic.com/environment/habitats/water-pressure/#page=1 [accessed March 2011].

In December 2007, the Secretary-General of the United Nations, Ban Ki Moon, told a conference that population growth, rising consumption, pollution and poor management of water could even lead to wars between nations. He said:

> Throughout the world, water resources continue to be spoiled, wasted and degraded. The consequences for humanity are grave. Water scarcity threatens economic and social gains and is a potent fuel for wars and conflict.

A separate report identified 46 countries, with a combined population of 2.7 billion people, where climate change and water-related crises could create a high risk of violent conflict.[9]

Arable Land and Food Supplies

Available agricultural land is scarcely sufficient even to meet the current needs of the population, while the global population could rise by as much as 50 per cent in the next half-century. It is unlikely that the amount of arable land can be significantly increased in that time. Higher agriculture demand may require higher levels of irrigation and energy, yet food production is already demanding of resources, requiring several times more externally provided energy than the energy content of the food itself.[10] The food riots in recent years may be just a taste of more serious political upheaval to come. Millions of people have been affected, and have protested, in countries such as Bolivia, Peru, Haiti, Ivory Coast, Burkina Faso, Ethiopia, Bangladesh, Cambodia, Thailand and the Philippines. In one example in 2008, around 20,000 textile workers in Bangladesh protested after the price of rice in the country had doubled in the previous year, threatening serious hunger for workers earning a monthly salary of around $25. One-off events, such as the drought in Russia and the Ukraine in 2010, can exacerbate matters. Arguably, speculation in food prices also contributes to volatility and unmanageable price rises.[11] Food price inflation was a factor behind the North African uprisings that began in early 2011, indicating the potential for pressure on arable land to lead to major political upheaval.

Energy

In 1973, during an outbreak of fighting in the Arab–Israeli war, the oil price soared, creating high inflation and economic recession in much of the industrialised world. Similar problems erupted just a few years later during the Iranian revolution of 1979.

---

9   Water shortages are likely to be a trigger for wars, says UN chief Ban Ki Moon, *The Times*, 4 December 2007.

10   Kullander, Sven, Food Security: Crops for People, not Cars, *Ambio: A Journal of the Human Environment*, Volume 39, Number 3, 249–256, DOI: 10.1007/s13280-010-0032-5.

11   Amid mounting food crisis, governments fear revolution of the hungry, Bill van Auken, *Global Research*, April 30 2008.

These episodes exposed the vulnerability of major economies to the price of a single commodity, and ought to have prompted major investment in alternative energy sources. The technology existed. Recent initiatives on, for example, wave and tidal power for electricity generation, do not rely on new inventions – the engineering capability existed back in the 1970s. It is a mystifying and historic failure of political leadership, especially in the west, that the opportunity was not seized to develop clean energy sources, as well as radical improvements to insulation and building design. The geo-political benefits would have been immense: reduced imports; reduced revenues to state sponsors of terrorism such as Libya; cleaner environments for citizens and wildlife; lower risk of damage to tourism and fishing industries from spills; lower business and domestic energy bills, in turn reducing social security costs that have added so much to fiscal deficits in recent years.

What should have been done 30 years ago, however, can be done now, but there is much less time available. Some experts project an energy crunch within the next decade or so; even before the Japanese nuclear crisis, where four power plants had to be decommissioned following damage in the earthquake and tsunami on 10 March 2011. The disaster prompted other countries to reconsider their commitment to new nuclear power stations.[12]

It is unsustainable that something as fundamental as energy supply could depend on a finite resource. Promising developments on increasing the productivity of solar power, and tapping new sources of energy, need to be encouraged. It is easy to find sceptics to the renewables agenda, but what is striking is that some countries are far in advance of others. Israel, for example, aims to be carbon-free by 2020. The Timna Renewable Energy Park in the Negev Desert, announced in 2009, will generate up to 200MW of power, from solar, wind and production of biogas from municipal waste. This builds on the country's established hi-tech research and business clusters. The Eilat-Eilot Renewable Energy Authority plans to turn the southern desert into a 'Silicon Valley' of clean energy, encouraging innovation to improve the amount of power that can be generated from renewable sources.[13]

IN SUMMARY

Reviewing the stark evidence of the debt burden, the ageing society and the environmental crunch points that are rapidly approaching, it is possible to become

---

12   Nuclear renaissance threatened as Japan's reactor suffers, Bloomberg News, 13 March 2011.
13   The 2010 Eilat-Eilot Renewable Energy Conference looks to carbon-free future, i-Planet Energy Industry News, 6 November 2009. Available at: http://iplanetenergynews. com/index.php/2009/11/06/the-2010-eilat-eilot-renewable-energy-conference-looks-to-carbon-free-energy/ [accessed 28 October 2012].

daunted or depressed. Corporate leaders can feel alienated from the agenda when it is dominated by extremist voices that lump all businesses together as evil agents of the forces of 'globalisation'. They can also assume that one has to compromise the profit motive in order to attend to matters of social responsibility. The reasons for this lie in the ideological malaise of the past few decades: the failure of neo-liberalism to meet human needs, and the failure of the left to produce an alternative. In order to construct a more practical, optimistic agenda, it is necessary to unpick some of the misleading beliefs that led us to crisis. Business leaders can and should be part of the solution: they have far more to offer than most other constituencies. Unfortunately, they have been held prisoner by a toxic ideology that, for the past 40 years, has promoted the view that possessing a conscience and seeking a profit are mutually exclusive. The next chapter provides an analysis of how this occurred.

CHAPTER 3

THE MYTHS THAT HOLD US BACK

One of the most influential trends in recent years has been the emerging popularity of 'behavioural economics'. It follows the failure of mathematical risk models in the run-up to the credit crisis, and the awarding in 2002 of the Economics Nobel Prize to a psychologist, Daniel Kahneman, whose experiments have indicated that people do not make economic decisions in rational ways.

To some satirical commentators, behavioural economics is no more than ancient common sense. Writing in *The Times* in December 2010, Philip Collins claimed that this 'new' discipline simply assigns psychological jargon to well-known observations. Examples include knowing that we like a drink even though we'll get a hangover (over-discounting the future) or that we're scared things will go wrong (loss-aversion). He quipped that Kahneman 'got a Nobel prize for proving stuff that old ladies say in the post office'.[1]

The piece was engagingly witty. What this observation lacks, however, is a sense of context. The reason that professional economics has had to reacquaint itself with the blindingly obvious is that, for the past 40 years, its guiding principles have been the opposite. Even fairly basic observations about human behaviour disappeared from consideration in mainstream economic theory, because it was based on the notions either that people don't exist, or that we are unthinking acquisitive machines. A mechanistic metaphor has been common, in which money supply determined inflation, or in which corporations were 'leveraged' or 're-engineered'. People became 'human resources', and their motivations divorced from strategic consideration, placed in a separate category, hived off to the HR department and consigned to a single, patronising paragraph in the annual report about 'the most important asset', without acknowledgement of the fact that this precious asset also happens to generate all the others.

Institutional governance has gone badly wrong in the past couple of decades. If something has gone awry in practice, it is likely to be based on flawed theory. This

---

1   Collins, Philip, A White Paper won't stop my mum smoking, *The Times*, 3 December 2010.

chapter is an attempt to retrace the ideological steps, as a means of encouraging enquiry into a better way of understanding how economies and organisations behave in real life.

A first step is to recognise that the term 'behavioural economics' is not a separate discipline from mainstream economics. Rather, the phrase is tautological in nature. All economics is determined by human decisions, that is, behaviour. There is no other kind. Financial data is no more or less than a by-product of human conduct. This is both screamingly obvious, and institutionally denied – a classic 'Emperor's new clothes' phenomenon.

Probably the most significant event in the popularising of the ideas behind the orthodoxy that behaviour could be overlooked in economics and management was the publication in 1970 in the *New York Times* of a seminal article by economist Milton Friedman, of the hugely influential Chicago School. It set out the beliefs behind the framework and attitudes behind corporate governance for the following four decades: that the shareholders 'own' the company; that the corporation is just a vehicle for maximising their returns; that to attend to social or environmental concerns is 'socialism' and that measurement of performance is by the financial bottom line.[2]

By the 2000s, serious questions were emerging in business schools about this philosophy. One of the most thorough and articulate critiques was penned by the late Sumantra Ghoshal, and published shortly after his untimely death of a brain haemorrhage in 2004. Called 'Bad Management Theories are Destroying Good Management Practices', and published in the *Academy of Management Learning & Education*, it traces the development of amoral, misanthropic notions that have caused so much economic damage in recent decades. It clinically exposes some historic errors, and is an honest confession that business schools and the management discipline had been complicit. In this chapter, we highlight some of the most damaging phenomena:

- physics envy;
- agency theory;
- a misreading of politics; and
- a misunderstanding of the nature of interdependence.

PHYSICS ENVY

In trying to establish management as a 'science', business theory imported the principles from the physical sciences, but dangerously overlooked the differences,

---

2   Friedman, Milton, The social responsibility of business is to increase its profits, *New York Times* magazine, 13 September 1970.

replacing, in the words of Ghoshal, 'all notions of human intentionality with a firm belief in causal determinism for explaining all aspects of corporate performance'. He added:

> *In effect, we have professed that business is reducible to a kind of physics in which even if individual managers do play a role, it can safely be taken as determined by ... economic social and psychological laws.*[3]

A similar case is made in Bent Flyvbjerg's *Making Social Science Matter*,[4] published in 2001, in which he argued that an attempt to use the methodology of the physical sciences in the social sphere is a historic error. People are not simply acted upon; we also act. And this goes way beyond instinct for survival; we have a conscience and free will. Economics is not therefore modellable like process control dynamics of an engineering system such as a chemical plant. Formal economics ventured too far down the path of assuming that it could be. Raymond Tallis, a neuroscientist, is another prominent thinker who has warned of recent trends to deny the free will and conscience of human individuals as sentient beings. He complains of a tendency 'to deny the role of mind, of self-conscious agency, in human affairs'.[5]

Moreover, as management academic and author Gordon Pearson points out, the very presence of a theory that is widely adopted will itself have an effect on the way in which human affairs are run. This is a crucial difference with the physical sciences: an astronomer does not affect the movement of the planets and the stars by looking at them. Pearson says:

> *Management theory pretends to be scientific. If you develop a scientific theory, it doesn't affect the facts. But if you develop an economic theory, it can be accepted by people, who will operate accordingly. So it will affect realities.*[6]

WITCHCRAFT, MESMERISM AND AGENCY THEORY

From time to time in the development of human knowledge and expertise, an illogical practice with no basis in evidence gains widespread acceptance and remains acceptable for decades or even centuries, supported by eminent figures from the professions and academe. Theology developed the theory of witchcraft, medical science produced blood-letting and mesmerism. Economics gave us agency theory.

3   Ghoshal, Sumantra, Bad Management Theories are Destroying Good Management Practices, *Academy of Management Learning & Education*, Volume 4, Number 1, 75–91, 2005.
4   Flyvbjerg, Bent, *Making Social Science Matter*, Cambridge University Press, 2001.
5   Tallis, Raymond, Escape from Eden, *The New Humanist*, Volume 118, Number 4, November–December 2003.
6   Pearson, Gordon, *The Road to Co-operation: Escaping the Bottom Line*, Gower Publishing, 2012.

Unlike the superstitions listed above, however, this practice remains very much in use, causing avoidable damage to otherwise quite healthy organisations.

When describing the comprehensive wrongness of agency theory, it is difficult to know where to begin. It doesn't even pass the basic threshold of the awkward question by an intelligent child. A theory devised to counter the negative side-effects of a bad hire to an executive position doesn't even consider the option of making a good one. It takes assumptions about human nature that are both unproven and inconsistent with everyday observations: that we are short-termist, opportunistic, calculating, amoral, without a conscience or even much in the way of free will. It is a tiny fraction of an improvement on re-engineering metaphors, given that at least it permits the existence of human beings; but such is the reductive, pessimistic assumption around human nature it makes that the achievement is negligible.

The so-called 'agency problem' is defined on the basis that it is the primary intention of every individual appointed to a senior post in a corporation to harm the interests of shareholders, line his or her pockets in opportunistic ways, before escaping with the cash. This is accompanied by the equally incorrect assertion that stockholders own the company. They don't – they own shares in the company, and benefit from limited liability. As Ghoshal points out, the stockholder is no more of a valid stakeholder in the company than the employees. Moreover, in an age where capital is more freely available than skills, stockholders are less important to the typical corporation than human capital. They are also more mobile.[7] So the Friedmanite approach hits some basic practical problems, as well as being logically flawed.

Yet the theory has prompted development of elaborate schemes of sticks and carrots in which stock holding has featured strongly, and tenures of executives encouraged to be short, with minimal levels of cooperation between the CEO and the chair. The idea is that an executive has to be incentivised to operate in the shareholders' interest; that he or she cannot be trusted to manage the corporation.

Agency theory isn't even consistent with the equally cynical, but rather different assumption about reward for junior people. As one of us has noted in a previous report, one of the more influential theories in reward systems for junior staff has been that of Herzberg. This 'two-factor' theory asserts that pay and conditions do not form the main motivating factor; they are essential as a 'hygiene' factor. The motivators are achievement, recognition and the work itself.

Taken together, however, agency and 'hygiene' theories meant that we have had the orthodoxy that for executives, money is supposed to be the sole motivator; for

7   Ghoshal, Sumantra, Bad Management Theories are Destroying Good Management Practices, *Academy of Management Learning & Education*, Volume 4, Number 1, 75–91, 2005.

junior people, it does not motivate at all! Not only is this inconsistent, one would have thought that a pay rise would, if anything, make more material difference to the quality of life for a low-income than a high-income individual.[8]

Gordon Pearson, author of *The Rise and Fall of Management*,[9] and *The Road to Co-operation*,[10] is an outspoken critic of agency theory. He says:

> *If you accept the twentieth Century version of maximising own interest, that explains the thinking behind agency theory: the idea that executives were the agents of shareholders; that they were trying to screw the shareholders and everyone else, therefore the shareholders have an 'agency problem': directors working for their own interest. The word 'shirking' is the term they use. None of these economists' ideas have ever really worked in the real company.*

He believes that no effective manager is likely to be able to operate agency theory in the real world, but that it has unfortunately had an impact, in the realm of the self-fulfilling prophesy. By deliberately weakening the trust between stockholders and the board, and between the board and the executive, CEOs and other senior directors may be tempted to look to their own interest and more at the short term. Empirical evidence suggests, however, that the more successful hires are those who, like Paul Polman at Unilever, Robin Saxby at ARM, and those whose case studies we feature in this book, support the long-term sustainability and profitability of the organisation as the central task of the senior executive, based on an understanding of the huge overlap of interests between different stakeholders.

Another baleful legacy of agency theory is the widespread notion of the 'independent' board director. This is a fictional concept, contrary to the principles of governance and company law. It arises from the cynical assumptions around the 'agency problem', in which an 'independent' board director is supposed to be more likely to police the inherently opportunistic, sly and selfish motivations of the director, because they are less likely to be in collusion.

In law, however, if you are a director, you are not independent. The simple fact of being contracted by an organisation means that you are not a disinterested party; indeed, it has never been explained why this should be an advantage. The responsibility of each and every director is the long-term stewardship of the organisation. There is no distinction between executive and non-executive – each

---

8   Whiteley, Philip, ed., Strategic Risk & Reward: Integrating Reward Systems and Business Strategies after the Credit Crisis, *International Financing Review*, 2008.

9   Pearson, Gordon, *The Rise and Fall of Management: A Brief History of Practice, Theory and Context*, Gower Publishing, 2009.

10   Pearson, Gordon, *The Road to Co-operation: Escaping the Bottom Line*, Gower Publishing, 2012.

board member has equal status and responsibilities. In the UK, this principle was re-established as recently as the Company Act 2006. No director is an agent of the stockholder, in common sense, in business sense or in law. It is a fiction dreamt up by the Chicago School.

Agency theory has strongly influenced reviews of codes of governance around the world, including by the Securities & Exchange Commission in the US, the Higgs Review in the UK and by the Narayanamurthy Committee in India.[11] Features include an emphasis on 'independent' non-executive board directors, and separation of chief executive and board chairman role – a more understandable desire, but a judgement that depends heavily upon institutional context. The unspoken assumption behind agency theory and these reviews is that the primary role of the board is as a policeman to protect shareholder interests against devious actions by the executive. The alternative of a stewardship function for the board, honouring its legal contract to oversee good management of the company, is not considered, yet this is the healthier version that we have observed and will promote in this book, illustrated with case studies.

All of the above does not mean that executives naturally tend towards noble, uplifting aspirations for the long-term health of the organisation and society, only to be brought down by the practice of agency theory. CEOs can be inspiring, enlightened leaders who transform the lives of their employees and customers, while generating strong profits and aiding society. They may also turn out to be psychopathic; fraudulent or even violent. Agency theory, peddling its assumptions about rational calculation and the short term, misses both. It arbitrarily focuses on a narrow range of human behaviours that, in the real world, are actually quite rare. The recognition that the leadership role is both important, and for the long term, needs to be based on a proper recognition of how leaders actually behave, based on the long-established literature, not just recent publications by Henry Mintzberg, Sumantra Ghoshal, Jeffrey Pfeffer and Lynda Gratton, but also the Hawthorne experiments of the 1920s–1930s and ultimately the thoughts of Aristotle on practical wisdom. The inter-war years, nearly a century ago, were a particularly fertile period for development of research, ideas and practice around strong organisational leadership. Richard Kwiatkowski of Cranfield University has pointed out that many of the current principles of leadership were well established nearly a century ago, though often with different terminology. And a little while before this period, the remarkable speaker and author Mary Parker Follett (1868–1933) demonstrated the importance of communication, intelligent leadership and harnessing informal networks within the complexity of the enterprise. What an historic tragedy that Milton Friedman, not Mary Parker Follett, has been the most influential figure on contemporary management practice in the past century!

---

11   Ghoshal, Sumantra, Bad Management Theories are Destroying Good Management Practices, *Academy of Management Learning & Education*, Volume 4, Number 1, 75–91, 2005.

MISREADING OF POLITICS, AND BUSINESS PROCESS RE-ENGINEERING

An important dimension in the development of ideas around governance and economics is politics. Milton Friedman warned that those considering other stakeholders, even to the most token degree, were preaching 'pure and unadulterated socialism'. He aired this view in the *New York Times* article referred to earlier. It was in 1970, during the Cold War, and not long after the McCarthy investigations in the 1950s into alleged Communist infiltration into US institutions. The article is astonishingly extreme and doctrinaire. It is also loosely phrased. For example, he wrote that: 'Only "people" have responsibilities ... "Business" as a whole cannot be said to have responsibilities, even in this vague sense' (The inverted commas are Friedman's, and are not justified or explained). This convoluted sentence is a non-sequitur; it assumes that business does not consist of people. At best it can produce muddled practice; at worst, highly dangerous approaches. One can see the accounting scandals and banking crisis of the early twenty-first century in the making.

The socialism reference is highly relevant, however, in the light of subsequent events. The Cold War was not just one of military rivalry between two superpowers, but also a competition between competing economic systems. So when the Berlin Wall fell in 1989, and the widespread poverty and inefficiency behind the former Iron Curtain became more apparent, it was clear that the West had a superior economic system. It was widely assumed that this made Friedman correct – but this has turned out to be simplistic thinking. To begin with, it pays too high a regard to the alternative in the east: if something is less bad than Soviet Communism, does that make it good? It is a pretty low threshold. Moreover, although Friedman's view was dominant, there was diversity in approaches in the west. Many good corporate citizens who emphasised being a good employer were also among the most profitable companies: Southwest Airlines, WL Gore & Associates, JCB and John Lewis in the UK, for example. So a huge proportion of the wealth generated in the west was by corporations who followed a very different philosophy from Friedman's.

What happened after 1989 however, probably as a by-product, was the explosion of popularity in the most materialistic, narrowly defined interpretation of Friedman's orthodoxy. In the early 1990s, immediately after the fall of Communism, 'business process re-engineering' became all the rage, trying to reduce a complex organisation to a set of processes. Instead of subconsciously eliminating the people, this was done openly and with pride. In the case of some organisations, there probably was over-staffing and underperformance, and the rapid development in IT could lead to significant gains from automation. But using a model of a corporation as little more than a collection of processes led to oversimplification and waste. Reducing staff to a 'cost', with no analysis of the value of the skills and teamwork that are needed in the real world to make any business process work, was a fatal error. During the

1990s, Friedman's ideas became more popular, even though a body of research was being built up indicating that the companies that performed the best, including on financial measures, emphasised high levels of commitment and staff engagement, rather than slavish devotion to the bottom line and maximising shareholder value. By the end of the decade, business author Jeffrey Pfeffer commented on the 'very strange' phenomenon of business theory moving in an opposite direction to the evidence base.[12]

The misanthropic biases in management orthodoxy, especially business process re-engineering and the use of the term 'human resources', have bred much cynicism towards corporations, and especially the banks, in recent decades, depriving legitimate and ethically-run corporations of the social support that they merit and need. The actual or apparent greed and disregard for society or the environment of the more obvious corporate villains of the past decade is an obvious factor behind this cynicism and suspicion. Another is the dense jargon and mystique that has grown up in some circles, especially finance, accompanying the cults of 'total shareholder return' and 'business process re-engineering'. Yet this has occluded the fact that the core measures, the quarterly report, are mono-dimensional and crude.

An irony is that the more sophisticated approaches to management based on sustainability, and a recognition of the complexity of contributions of different stakeholders, are concepts that are easier to grasp for politicians, employees and society than the crude devotion to total shareholder return. It's rooted in the real world, not accountancy. There is less jargon. Executives talk about customer experience rather than synergistic growth; about creating new services rather than leveraging assets. One of the many admirable aspects to Paul Polman's address in November 2010 was its clarity. No, he wasn't going to appease the manipulators of hot money, and he wasn't going to apologise for this. Such plain speaking is refreshing. Most Mondays, in the *Financial Times*, Lucy Kellaway devotes her column to satirising pretentious management language. She even created a superb comic vehicle to illustrate the case – the fictional soap opera character Martin Lukes, dedicated to his synergistic visions furthering his vision in the integethical space, and so on.

Such jargon is largely a by-product of the domination of accountancy, which almost forces executives to use euphemism, because the very concept of management based on accountancy is an inversion of reality. Referring to the real people you actually have to work with and serve as 'intangible', and pretending that the arbitrary estimations of book value in the accounts are 'tangible' means you are already one foot inside fantasy-land. Rescuing the company from such illogical biases can also assist us in adopting plain language rather than pretension and cant.

---

12   Pfeffer, Jeffrey, *The Human Equation*, Harvard Business Publishing, 1998.

INTERDEPENDENCE IS A REALITY, NOT JUST AN IDEA

A feature of both political thought and agency theory is a tendency to assume that different constituencies are inevitably at war with one another. The board is trying to police the executive; the unions wish to secure gains from management; the executives are trying to bear down on costs. Now, it is an absolute basic principle of all business relationships, even where levels of trust and respect are high, that the interests of different parties are not the same. This does not, however, mean that they are always in inherent conflict. They are never the *same*; but they nearly always overlap. Business orthodoxy in recent decades has, in our view, vastly overemphasised the potential for conflict, and understated or ignored the degree of interdependence.

In the real world, nothing gets achieved without high levels of cooperation within organisations, and between corporations and suppliers. We need to rethink the organisation. It is not a set of assets, one of which is 'people'. This is wrong in theory and in fact. Rather, an organisation is a complex web of relationships, between individuals and teams, internally and externally. As services become more complex, environmental protection becomes more urgent, and skill levels higher, the level of interdependence actually increases. In fact, there is almost nothing you can achieve on your own. The ability to communicate, including in geographically dispersed groups, and to work effectively as a team; having open discussions, making compromises, sharing information and getting to know one another, and so on, are business essentials, not optional 'soft skills'. If you talk with any successful business executive or entrepreneur, they talk intensively about the importance of getting the right hires, engaging in deep conversation to ensure there is a joint understanding and vision, and nurturing engagement to the task.

Above all, the biggest myth is the assumption that ethical concerns are inherently at war with the profit motive. This can lead to a binary delusion (see Chapter 1), in which one is supposed to have to choose between head and heart. The case studies we present in this book illustrate that it is possible for more than one stakeholder to benefit simultaneously. The term 'win–win' has started to appear in management in recent years. It is jargon, but a rare case of good jargon.

IN SUMMARY

In business management, bad theory has led to bad practice. It has been based on conceptual errors: that the company consists of assets, that costs are mono-dimensional, that it's only the stockholders who matter, and so on. These errors are easy to identify and correct (see boxed text on the following page for a summary).

Human beings are intelligent and adaptable. We can do much, much better than this, and the best organisations are already doing so. We hope that the ideas presented in this book encourage a view of the organisation that is at once more optimistic and more practical than the damaging notions that have been fashionable in recent decades.

SOME COMMON BUSINESS MYTHS, AND SOME BETTER IDEAS TO REPLACE THEM

The company is a collection of assets, one of which is people.

The company is a collection of teams of people, who generate assets.

The chief executive has only one objective: to maximise shareholder returns.

The chief executive has multiple objectives: to serve the customer, to encourage innovation, to create opportunities for staff, ensure organisational sustainability, behave responsibly and generate returns for all stakeholders, including shareholders.

Environmental protection is an ethical luxury; an optional extra for the commercially minded executive team.

Environmental protection is an inescapable duty for all executives, for commercial as well as ethical reasons.

Driving down direct costs boosts business performance.

Understanding business costs is a complex matter, depending on an understanding of human behaviour. It is helpful to have a measure of the value generated by different teams, as well as the aggregate cost in employing them.

FURTHER READING

Ghoshal, Sumantra, Bad Management Theories are Destroying Good Management Practices, *Academy of Management Learning & Education*, Volume 4, Number 1, 75–91, 2005.

Pearson, Gordon, *The Rise and Fall of Management: A Brief History of Practice, Theory and Context*, Gower Publishing, 2009.

Pearson, Gordon, *The Road to Co-operation: Escaping the Bottom Line*, Gower Publishing, 2012.

Pfeffer, Jeffrey, *The Human Equation*, Harvard Business Publishing, 1998.

Mintzberg, Henry, *Managers not MBAs*, Financial Times Prentice Hall, 2004.

Impact of People Management Practices on Business Performance, Institute of Personnel & Development/University of Sheffield 1997. This concluded that:

> *Even more dramatic are the comparisons with other management practices, including use of competitive strategies, quality focus and investment in*

research & development. None of these ... appear to have anything like the same effect on performance as people management.

Much research on the links between high-performance workplaces and better business results has been carried out by Mark Huselid. See http://www.markhuselid. com/index.html

CHAPTER 4

BEYOND THE BALANCE SHEET

Every financial collapse is really just an ethical collapse that happened a few years earlier.

Umair Haque, *Harvard Business Review*

In Chapter 3, we discussed how the cult of maximising shareholder value was a narrow and unhelpful way of defining capitalism. It was described in an influential article in 1970 by one of the most eminent economists of the time, and became dominant for a long period after the tumultuous events of 1989.

Underneath this, however, was a very different strand of business management; one that rarely hit the headlines because, after all, good news is not news. This alternative philosophy might be described as stakeholder capitalism; an approach based on a commitment to engagement of all parties involved in an enterprise, including employees, customers and suppliers, and in an increasing number of cases respect for environmental sustainability. It does not apply to a particular organisational structure; it is more a culture and a style of leadership which, in our combined experience, we have come across in listed companies, privately owned companies, mutual societies and the non-profit sector.

Describing in an abstract sense the dynamics of the 'virtuous circle' in which enlightened leaders harness the shared interests of diverse stakeholders can sound ambitious – almost utopian. Yet it is exactly the way in which some of the most resilient and successful businesses organise themselves. Some of the organisations following this approach have been heavily influenced by leading thinkers, while others simply follow the pragmatic good sense of their enlightened founders. Examples in this latter category are WL Gore & Associates, Southwest Airlines and the Indian Tata company. Indeed, Tata does not so much depart from the 'total shareholder returns' philosophy as invert it completely. The founder J.N. Tata stated: 'In a free enterprise, the community is not just another stakeholder in business, but it is in fact the very purpose of its existence'.[1]

---

1   A good recent profile of Tata can be found in the spring 2010 edition, issue 58, of *Strategy & Business*. The article is titled 'Too Good to Fail' by Ann Graham.

There has been theory as well behind the stakeholder approach. One of the most influential thinkers in the development of this in the twentieth century was W. Edwards Deming, who influenced numerous organisations, principally manufacturers. He is often called the father of the 'quality movement', but this understates his achievements. It was not just about attention to quality on the production line, but rather a radically different philosophy to the whole concept of management, and what an organisation is for.

Some of the organisations to benefit from this teaching were Intel, Colgate-Palmolive, Harley Davidson, Procter & Gamble and Marshall Industries, as well as some of the most successful Japanese manufacturers such as Nissan and Toyota.

Deming's ideas are often taught in a completely separate module, or course, from ideas around total shareholder value or business process re-engineering. It is tacitly assumed that the two strands are complementary. We would argue that the two are fundamentally different, even opposed. Of Deming's famous 14 principles of organisational management, eight relate to teamwork, or engagement; for example 'driving out fear from the workplace'. This is very different from the approach of Milton Friedman, who said that to attend to social or environmental concerns is 'socialism' and that measurement of performance is by the financial bottom line (see Chapter 3). For Deming, the 'bottom line' was not a tool for performance measurement at all, but rather a by-product of attention to quality, teamwork and an understanding of the customer's needs. Unfortunately, the richness of his ideas, and particularly his emphasis on teamwork and driving out fear, have often been downplayed, and his philosophy oversimplified to a set of guidance on quality control, sometimes called 'total quality management' or TQM.

Several decades after the peak of Deming's influence, in the late 1990s, Jeffrey Pfeffer observed that the trends in management practice were actually moving *away* from the evidence base, and seemed to be based more on Friedman's principles. Pfeffer has set out a newer evidence base of the practices of successful companies, and concluded that 'conventional wisdom is wrong'. He strongly criticises management by fad, or by simplistic mantra, and his research indicates that the most successful companies operate on the following principles:

- employment security;
- selective hiring of new personnel;
- self-managed teams and decentralisation of decision making as the basic principles of organisational design;
- comparatively high compensation contingent on organisational performance;
- extensive training;
- reduced status distinctions and barriers, including dress, language, office arrangements and wage differences across levels;

- extensive sharing of financial and performance information throughout the organisation.[2]

Every single principle relates to people management and culture; similar to Deming's findings and to the empirical findings we can deduce from Tata, WL Gore and so on. As we noted in the last chapter, all economics is behavioural. Yet, as we noted in the Introduction, this recognition does not reach the senior executive suite in governments or in many corporations. Some of the most important leadership research does not influence our most important leadership decisions. Instead, they are made on projections based on the most recent results of growth or profit, or on curbing the most easily measurable costs, or altering the structure of the organisation or government department.

This bias is seen in the reaction to Paul Polman's announcement of Unilever's commitment to sustainability. It was met more favourably than might have been the case before the credit crisis, but there was still some scepticism, for example in the *Financial Times*. In a climate in which the findings and principles of sound leadership were the norm, the onus would be more on executives departing from such practices and pursuing short-termist policies to justify their approach.

BOOSTING THE BUSINESS CAN HELP SOCIETY

What about profits and the shareholder, however; and what about the short term? Organisations do need to consider these. Leadership is difficult and concentrating on the long term is not enough in itself – the organisation needs profits in the short run also. These are essential considerations, but they are not in opposition to the recognition that all economics is behavioural and that leadership of people is always central. We would argue that the degree of interdependence between different stakeholders in a business has been historically understated (see Chapter 3), so the potential for realising commercial aims and people's aspirations simultaneously is too often unexplored.

It is common that businesses seeking to improve service for purely business reasons end up creating considerable social benefits. For example, in the mid-2000s the UK branch of the Danish facilities giant ISS had discovered a problem in some of its units with staff turnover, which had an impact on service, and also resulted in high costs through heavy use of recruitment agencies and management time attending to departure of employees and induction of new staff. Senior managers identified that some units had much higher staff turnover than others, particularly of recent hires. Detailed exit interviews teased out some of the problems, around pay and career prospects, and measures were taken to remedy some of these complaints. It was also found that recruits who had been recommended by current employees were

---

2   Pfeffer, Jeffrey, *The Human Equation*, Harvard Business Press, 1998.

more likely to stay longer and perform better, so a scheme to incentivise referrals by staff was introduced. The first year yielded £380,000 savings on agency fees alone, while lower staff turnover reduced indirect costs and boosted service levels. The company then invested in training, creating a stronger career path for individuals.[3] Many of the workers were immigrants on relatively low pay in jobs such as cleaning and catering, probably in many cases remitting hard currency home. So with the opening up of better pay and prospects, opportunities were opened up for thousands of families to break out of poverty.

Initiatives designed primarily for commercial purposes have had a tremendous social benefit, potentially transformational for many individuals. There is no compromise with the profit motive; on the contrary, motivated staff with good career prospects generally deliver a much better service, more than paying for the investment made in them. Moreover, some of these investments – for example, exit interviews – are modest; and some of the returns – for example, lower agency costs – are relatively short term. So being ethical in a commercial way is not necessarily a case of grand gestures and long-term visions; it can be applied common sense based on an understanding of the needs of customers and of staff. It includes recognition that while cost control is, of course, of paramount importance; cost is actually a by-product of human behaviour. Costs go up or down depending not only on how much you are paying your staff, but how they are performing. Seemingly minor matters – such as how courteously service staff deal with customer queries – can have a bigger impact on profit and loss than the more easily measurable costs of heating, lighting and wages.

Marks & Spencer, the UK retail giant, approached the matter more from the desire to be more ethical, but as the case study below illustrates, it has been 'pleasantly surprised' by the business benefits of creating better career opportunities for its factory workers in Bangladesh, and other ethical initiatives. ISS began with a commercial perspective, but created considerable social benefits for their employees. From different starting points, the outcomes were remarkably similar. This illustrates the considerable overlap of interest between owners and workers.

CASE STUDY

Marks & Spencer: Sustainability and a Living Wage Background

Marks & Spencer is a leading UK-based retailer, principally in food and clothing. It employs 75,000 people in 30 countries, has more than 600 stores in the UK and 300 overseas, and around 25 million customers. In 2007, the then chief executive of Marks & Spencer, Sir

---

3   Reported at the meetings of the Human Capital Forum, 24 October 2007 and 24 April 2008 (www.humancapitalforum.com) and in the document 'Making it Count: Human Capital Investments that Deliver Improved Business Performance', published by Logica, September 2009.

Stuart Rose, launched 'Plan A' (because there is no Plan B for the one planet we have), an ambitious sustainability programme for the retailer, covering environmental protection, eco-efficiency and support for the communities in which it operates. It established 100 initiatives as part of the plan, which it aimed to fulfil by 2012.

By March 2010, the company was able to report that Plan A had delivered on 46 of the 100 goals, and could report notable achievements, including the following in 2009–2010:

- cost savings of around £50m for M&S;
- new products and services, including 250,000 customers from M&S Energy;
- cut CO_2 emissions by 40,000 tonnes;
- recycled 2 million used garments via Oxfam;
- reduced 10,000 tonnes of packaging;
- diverted 20,000 tonnes of waste from landfill;
- saved 387 million food carrier bags;
- used 1,500 tonnes of recycled polyester (equivalent to 37 million bottles);
- saved 100 million litres of water;
- recycled or re-used over 130 million clothing hangers;
- raised £15m for charities.

At the same time, the firm announced a further 80 initiatives, designed to ensure the company becomes 'the world's most sustainable major retailer by 2015'. The new ambitions included:

- working with suppliers to provide training and education programmes – including in basic healthcare and workers' rights – for 500,000 workers in their factories;
- helping suppliers create 200 'Plan A' factories with either ethical or environmental features, or both, and encouraging 10,000 farmers who produce fresh foods for M&S to join the company's sustainable agriculture programme;
- becoming the first major retailer to ensure that six key raw materials it uses – palm oil, soya, cocoa, beef, leather, coffee – come from sustainable sources that do not contribute to deforestation, one of the biggest causes of climate change;
- increasing the number of clothing garments our customers recycle every year from two million to 20 million, including via the partnership with Oxfam, significantly reducing the tonnage of clothing sent to landfill.

    (More details are available on the M&S website, in the press announcement 1 March 2010: http://corporate.marksandspencer.com/media/press_releases)

Mike Barry, Head of Sustainable Business for Marks & Spencer, says that Plan A sprang initially from a 'moral imperative', but that the company has been pleasantly surprised by some of the business benefits.

> We felt that big business needed to be tackling the enormous social and environmental challenges. We are a values-driven business; but we are also aware that there is a business case. We had suspected that there might be [business benefits] we have been pleasantly surprised – it has been even better than we expected. The business case has been several-fold: eco-efficiency, less waste, lower energy, less packaging. There have been benefits on the productivity side, and there is a reputational benefit to the customer.

M&S is a commercial entity; it cannot jeopardise its viability by over-extending itself with social or environmental commitments. However, by intelligently identifying the overlapping concerns of employees, suppliers, shareholders, executives and customers, it has developed some innovative approaches which benefit all stakeholders.

With customers, for example, questions of convenience, cost and quality are not the only factors. Indeed, the extent to which M&S customers are green and ethical may surprise some observers. The company has found that this does extend to purchasing behaviour; it is not simply a case of claiming to be ethical in questionnaires.

In M&S customer surveys, the company segments its 25 million customers into four groups:

1.   About 10 per cent of its customers, and 9 per cent of the UK population, are passionately interested – they are very ethical, buy fair-trade, and so on.
2.   About 35 per cent of M&S customers, and 28 per cent of UK population, are 'light green'. They are concerned about these issues, but they don't want to pay more or sacrifice quality. They effectively say 'If you can do good stuff for no extra cost, we will prefer you to your competitors'.
3.   The third group, about 35 per cent of M&S customers, and 38 per cent of UK general population, are saying that they understand the green and social dimension, but they feel intimidated by the amount of change that's needed and feel they don't know where to start. They want to do one small thing a week, on the basis that everyone else does, so it makes a difference. So there is a kind of 'sustainable tribalism'. An example is plastic carrier bags: they are keen to stop using them if everyone else does.
4.   Around 20 per cent of M&S customers, and 25 per cent of the general population, are not interested in this agenda. They are driven by income. Typically they are the poorest sections of society and they have, not surprisingly, other priorities in their lives.

The tendency to emphasise these concerns has dipped during the recession, but only slightly, Mr Barry reports. He says:

> *The biggest priority for a lot of people is the economy and jobs, but people still define themselves in those four groups. They say that they expect the government and big business to pick up the slack on environmental action in a recession, when ordinary citizens may have more pressing concerns. But it still means that 80 per cent of our customers, in some shape or form, want us to be green, and that 10 per cent of them will push us to be even more so. The vast majority want us to make a difference.*

Has there been resistance or scepticism from shareholders and financial journalists?

> *Interestingly, when we launched Plan A four years ago – so named because there is no Plan B – Stuart Rose spoke with leading shareholders and said that it was the right thing to do and asked: 'Are you with me?' They were not against it. They see it as a proxy for good management in the real world. Now, we have gone back and could demonstrate that last year the policy made a £50 million contribution to profits. It is not a huge issue for the investment*

community, though to be fair to them they need companies to prove there is a business case.

We have a very sophisticated mode for the business case; a monthly dashboard, showing savings from less packaging, less waste, less energy. We provide green energy service to customers. And we are able to drive the business case.

In terms of internal management, non-financial indicators have equal status to the finances, he adds. 'To take the example of the Food division. Our suppliers have several hundred factories. For these we have a balanced scorecard: Commercial performance of the supplier; Quality; Innovation capacity; and sustainability – social and environmental performance.

Bangladesh: A Living Wage

As part of Plan A, Marks & Spencer has sought to deepen its commitment to social development. In particular, a pilot programme to boost wages for workers in its suppliers in Bangladesh has proved highly promising, and illustrates the virtuous circle that can be achieved by leadership that understands the interdependence that businesses depend upon.

Suppliers to M&S employ hundreds of thousands of workers around the world, and the company has insisted that they pay the local minimum wage. This policy has been backed up by audits and inspections. By 2008–2009, some of the development charities that advise M&S began asking the company to be more aspirational on the social side, rather than just carrying out audits to prevent the worst types of exploitation. 'They were asking us to consider social matters as being on the same level as environmental questions', says Mr Barry.

There was a nervousness that climate change was becoming dominant, and that social concerns are just as important. What if we could aspire to pay not just the minimum wage but a living wage? In Bangladesh the legal minimum wage, in many cases, isn't enough for a typical family to live on. We said OK – we would look at a living wage.

At first, there were nerves, about the cost implications: how could we pay more and not put up the price of our products and see the business hit? For a few months there was lots of head-scratching; lots of bright people considering the challenge. Krishnan Hundal, Director of Technology, who heads a department of 70 technologists, suggested we did a trial in three factories, to see what happens. We found three suppliers [in Bangladesh]. What we found was that, very rapidly, by improving worker training, management training and productivity-management of the factory – how it flows – we could free up the money to make it more productive, and free up the cash to pay workers more – 23 per cent more. It was an interesting virtuous circle.

We're not claiming it's perfect, but we are rolling it out to 30 factories in Bangladesh. That will unfold over the next year or so. This is a way of driving up wages without jeopardising the business. I would emphasise the word

---

'trial'. Once we have done that we will try to take it to other countries – such as India and Sri Lanka.

With the enhanced training and wages there is less absenteeism, less down-time sorting out disputes, better quality on all levels; these contribute to better productivity, he says.

The recognition that social and commercial objectives can be achieved simultaneously has also been recognised by many trade unionists. The British trade union Prospect has sought to encourage corporate social responsibility programmes at the organisations where it has membership and representation. It seeks to work with the grain of business, rather than make demands that could prove unaffordable in the market.

Beverley Hall, International Development Co-ordinator, says:

> *We do respect the business case. It has to be a reasonable approach, because the flip side to all of this is that if you're cancelling a contract people lose their jobs. We say: 'We would prefer you to be an ethical supplier. These are the things we would like to see. We can help you achieve them'.*

The union has used the United Nations' eight Millennium Development Goals as the framework for its social responsibility work (see following case study). Working with enlightened businesses can have a more lasting impact on people's lives. She observes:

> *It is through jobs that people work their way out of poverty. Not only are they then earning an income, but you could say they are being educated in that workplace, gaining access to clean water; a whole range of matters; maternal things; paying for their children to go to school. You start to see these benefits mushroom. By looking at the Millennium Development Goals organisations could contribute to those.*

DIFFICULT DECISIONS

These examples demonstrate that it is a myth that the interests of different stakeholders always clash. There is huge potential to seek solutions that represent a 'win' for more than one. Sometimes, however, tough decisions have to be made. A central part of leadership is the wisdom to make those distinctions. Organisations where the engagement of employees is a priority have two advantages over others when economic conditions are harsh. Firstly, they have a store of goodwill to draw upon to help the organisation through tough times, and are less likely to see talented people head for the exit. Secondly, a policy of making redundancies a last resort means that, when they do have to be made, they are more likely to be accepted, limiting the impact on morale and service.

For the organisation with enlightened leadership, innovation is continual, employee engagement is always a priority, the people and the business strategies are considered together as part of a unified approach. It is not utopia; it is fundamentally practical. With an understanding of the realities of interdependence, especially in a complex business world requiring high skills and teamwork, practical business common sense and an ethical outlook are natural partners.

CASE STUDY

Prospect the Trade Union
Background

Prospect is a trade union for scientists, engineers and related specialisms in the private and public sector in the UK, in sectors including agriculture, defence, energy, environment, heritage, shipbuilding and transport. It was formed in 2001 by the merger of the Institution of Professionals Managers and Specialists (IPMS) and the Engineers and Managers Association (EMA), and in 2010 merged with the Connect union, representing people in the communications industry. This took membership to around 122,000.

Corporate Responsibility

Many of Prospect's members, being from the scientific community, are acutely aware of the environmental pressures in the modern economy. According to Beverley Hall, International Development Co-ordinator at the union, pressure has built over recent years for the union to be thoroughly committed to ethical conduct both in the social and the 'green' sphere. As a trade union, it is strongly guided by resolutions at conference, and these have given a lead on matters such as an ethical supply chain – both for the union itself and the organisations where it has members, and on environmentally responsible conduct.

'It [this policy] has come about by the membership saying we should be doing more to raise awareness of these issues', says Ms Hall.

> *We then researched all of this and came up with the idea that corporate responsibility could in fact help develop the Millennium Development Goals.*

The Millennium Development Goals have been established by the United Nations, and set out eight anti-poverty measures to aim for, which are:

- end poverty and hunger;
- universal education;
- gender equality;
- child health;
- maternal health;
- combat HIV/AIDS;
- environmental sustainability; and
- global partnership.[1]

She adds:

---

1   See http://www.un.org/millenniumgoals/graphic.shtml

Companies do a lot of philanthropic stuff. We have been saying: What you are doing is great, but have you considered aligning that with the Millennium Development Goals? For example, not just building a well, but teaching someone to maintain it; not just building a school, but paying a teacher's salary. Looking at the Millennium Development Goals helps you choose the projects to support. There is one on environmental sustainability: everyone is doing that now. One is on global networks. A lot of organisations have a wealth of information and expertise that can benefit the developing world. Companies have done that: O2, and Coca Cola, for example. There is a lot of expertise in these companies and organisations that can contribute by knowledge exchange.

The union has taken measures to promote consistency of standards across supply chains, both in its own affairs and those of the organisations where it has representation. 'It's evident that, if you as an organisation have health and safety policy, you could start by asking suppliers about their health and safety; how many people have died in their factories?' says Ms Hall.

The consultative European Works Council at EDF Energy, which operates in 12 European countries, has put pressure on the company for such consistency. Works councils are mandatory for larger international firms operating in the European Union, and provide a forum for discussion between senior managers and staff. 'They make sure that what EDF is doing in one country they would do elsewhere', says Ms Hall.

For example, if the worker gets given safety boots in one country he or she doesn't have to buy them in another. The Council started to put pressure on EDF management about accountability, and making levels of accountability more robust.

There has been a positive response throughout the union, and with management teams at organisations where Prospect has membership, especially in the private sector. 'From our membership on the private sector, they get it; it's not a problem', says Ms Hall. 'On the public sector it has taken a while'.

Part of the problem with public sector supply chains is that rules designed to ensure value-for-money have limited the freedom to insist on certain social or environmental standards. This, however, is changing, Ms Hall reports.

Government departments have environmental sustainability targets. Part of that remit is to reduce carbon emissions. Our argument has been that if you are doing that on the green side you should do that on the social side: labour standards, fair pay and so on. Initially, we were told that the OGC [Office of Government Commerce in the UK] sets the policy, and that some European Union regulations impose restrictions. When you are writing procurement specifications you can't ask for that to be included – it gets tricky … [however] from January 2011 that has changed.

Laos: Social and Environmental Protection

One project where Prospect has helped to improve both social and environmental protection is a major hydro-electric project in Laos, south-east Asia. EDF, where Prospect has membership, is one of the partners of the consortium heading the project. Lee Parris, a Prospect member, health and safety engineer and employee at EDF Energy, went to Laos to audit the structure of the dam. He audited the project against corporate social responsibility standards criteria. He also looked directly at things like the indigenous people who had to be moved; provision for the workers on the construction site; provision for indigenous people still in the area; directly against the CSR criteria.

He identified an environmental problem around disruption to the river's course in the area; they are now doing things to mitigate. EDF were paying for a clinic, and he picked up some questions in relation to the doctors.

A GOOD JOB

One important finding from the diverse examples of ISS, Marks & Spencer and Prospect is that the most sustainable way out of poverty is a good job, with prospects. It has multiple benefits: the better wages have an obvious direct impact on quality of life; there is likely to be more opportunity to support children in education and further education; there is the role model to provide to children; and there is the self-esteem and pride that results. There is also a sense of progress and ambition that comes from a career that can encourage a dynamic or entrepreneurial attitude in the family and community. Good jobs reduce incentives for earning in the informal or criminal economy, and in this way help to bind communities together.

In 2007 the opinion survey specialist company Gallup carried out an ambitious 'world poll' to discover some of the motivating factors behind the aspirations of people from across the globe. The single most important, recurring request, from people of all ages, both genders and all backgrounds was expressed quite starkly: 'I want a good job'. This issues a challenge to traditional aid agencies, and government redistribution efforts: people want opportunities more than hand-outs. The role of business leaders might be more relevant to economic development and anti-poverty strategies than the role of non-governmental organisations (NGOs) or the welfare departments of governments, whose role might be more for ensuring a safety net.

ARE BUSINESS-PEOPLE THE NEW PROGRESSIVES?

A lead feature in the January 2011 edition of *Harvard Business Review* heralded the start of a new era of corporate responsibility, understanding of human networks and commitment to societal health. Co-authored by Michael Porter, arguably the most influential business thinker of the past few decades, and running to 7,500 words, it calls on company leaders to 'take the lead in bringing business and society back together'. It seeks to shifts business orthodoxy towards the concept of 'shared value', seeing employees as partners, not a cost. It is an overdue recognition, but a welcome and highly significant one. The article concludes:

> *The purpose of the corporation must be redefined as creating shared value, not just profit per se. This will drive the next wave of innovation and productivity growth in the global economy. It will also reshape capitalism and its relationship to society. Perhaps most important of all, learning how to create shared value is our best chance to legitimize business again.*[4]

The authors declare: 'The recognition is there among sophisticated business and thought leaders, and promising elements of a new model are emerging'. We would take issue with some of the analysis. To begin with, the approach is not new. It is the way in which numerous enlightened business leaders, such as Herb Kelleher of Southwest Airlines and Bill Gore of WL Gore & Associates, or executives of John Lewis in the UK, have always operated. Elements of the philosophy can be found in recent thinkers such as Jeffrey Pfeffer, and in mid to late twentieth-century writers such as Peter Drucker and W. Edwards Deming, while Mary Parker Follett was writing and talking about creating shared value a century ago. The authors have a tendency to refer to the decades of the 'total shareholder return' and the exclusive emphasis upon cost and returns to be a phase in the evolution of business management thinking, whereas we would regard it as an aberration. Nonetheless, the recognition is welcome, and potentially historic.

This article highlights a widespread myth in thinking on management, economics and politics: the idea that the profit motive and social motives are inherently at war with each other. This myth is promoted by the founders of the 'total shareholder value' approach to business, but also by their opponents. It rests on a profound misunderstanding of how profits are generated. Ironically, many anti-capitalist protestors share the view of Milton Friedman, supposedly their ideological opposite, that social responsibility is a 'cost' to a business that diminishes profits. What we have found is that this is not the case at all, as the case studies in this book amply demonstrate. The popular notion that the pressure for profits forces selfish, acquisitive, reckless and dangerous conduct is wrong; so is the idea that the absence of a profit motive automatically encourages socially progressive conduct, as we shall discuss further in the next chapter.

In the real business world, especially where customer service is paramount, and skill levels are high, gaining profits requires high levels of cooperation, empathy and sensitivity, while maintaining the corporate reputation essential for continued profitable service demands attention is paid to ethical concerns on sourcing, health and safety and environmental responsibility. It is not a simple cause-and-effect relationship – you can be ethical and unprofitable, and you can be unethical and profitable – but there are strong pressures to encourage better corporate behaviour, especially where reputation and long-term resilience are priorities.

---

4   Porter, Michael and Kramer, Mark R., The Big Idea: Creating Shared Value, *Harvard Business Review*, January 2011.

The Porter-Kramer article on shared value creation does not sit alone. There are other promising developments from recent years illustrating that the recognition of the interconnectedness of business constituencies, and the huge potential to achieve commercial and social outcomes simultaneously, is growing and widespread. It is not just a niche activity, and certainly not a fad. A few are listed below:

- As noted, major companies such as Unilever and Marks & Spencer are committed to a long-term value-creation approach which, in the words of Paul Polman 'is equitable, which is shared, which is sustainable', and openly discourage short-term investors.
- In December 2010, the influential credit ratings agency Moody's introduced talent management indicators – a form of human capital analysis. This means that companies will need to demonstrate the value in their workforce in order to maintain a good credit rating and be able to borrow at reasonable rates. This will encourage more thoughtful, long-term stewardship of a company's people and their talents.
- There has been an increase in management due diligence in private equity; for example, as outlined in David Cooper's book *Leadership Risk: A Guide for Private Equity and Strategic Investors.*[5]
- Behavioural finance – influenced among others by Nassim Nicholas Taleb, who has effectively demolished the theories that propped up mathematical modelling of the economy, and demonstrated how human behaviour determines all economic outcomes.
- Successful human capital funds – set up for example by Laurie Bassi in the US and by AXA in Europe. Bassi Investments Inc, since 2001; and the AXA Human Capital Fund, since 2007, have consistently beaten the market, illustrating the deep interconnectedness between people management and business effectiveness. Innovation in information technology is making human capital analysis – through which business leaders understand the links between certain people-related investments and business returns – more practicable.

The examples of business leadership that go beyond merely avoiding social harm, towards creating vehicles for social progress on ambitious programmes such as poverty-reduction and environmental protection, is historic. It opens up huge opportunities. As stated, business leaders potentially can have more social impact than anyone else, as they can create careers for people; they can have more environmental impact as they tend to operate on a bigger scale than NGOs. This development raises an intriguing thought: are business leaders the new progressives? Conventionally, the idea of being an activist for a better world has assumed to belong in the realm of the non-profit sector. But convention has been proven wrong in many dimensions,

---

5   Cooper, David, *Leadership Risk: A Guide for Private Equity and Strategic Investors*, John Wiley, 2010.

and we believe it is wrong in this. Examples recorded in this book promise to rewrite some of the cynical assumptions that have underwritten left-wing and right-wing orthodoxy, as we shall discuss further in following chapters.

IN SUMMARY

Recognising that business and social objectives can often be met together does not relegate social concerns to being a mere means to a commercial end. Rather, it reflects the reality that the interrelatedness of complex businesses means that one cannot be disentangled from the other. Economists, who have had the dominant influence on the practice of management in the past century, have underplayed this reality, or failed to analyse it altogether. Our experience coincides with that of Gordon Pearson, quoted in Chapter 1, who referred to the 'incomprehension' of business management on the part of the most influential economic thinkers – Adam Smith, Karl Marx and Milton Friedman.

What the examples highlighted in this chapter illustrate is the three-dimensional nature of the elements that create effective business results, whether gauged in social outcomes or measured on the financial bottom line. Simply focusing on the financials is insufficient – even for financial management. After the past decade of institutional and economic crises that were exacerbated or even caused by an excessive focus on the quarterly result, we have to conclude that this yardstick is not fit for purpose. You may not care about the environment or the workers, nor even possess a conscience, yet still recognise the hopeless inadequacy of 'the bottom line' for measuring results. Though we do still recommend both.

CHAPTER 5

INTO THE FUTURE – THE LEADERSHIP CHALLENGE

In the past few decades, a common call from IMF economists and other representatives of the neo-liberal community that there should be 'labour market reforms' in many countries to assist 'the supply side'. The idea is the following: if employers have their hands tied with too many legal restrictions on hiring and firing, it can be harder to match their staffing requirements to the real demands of the economy; or they can do so, but too slowly or at disproportionate cost. This can hamper economic and employment growth and wider development of an advanced economy. In some contexts, there is a strong case for such reform: where there are high levels of restrictive practices – such as bureaucratic union recognition laws, or unnecessarily strict licence requirements for certain professions.

Why is there never a call for 'management reform'? It is extraordinary to suppose that relatively low-paid workers, with little or no influence upon business strategy, should alone shoulder the burden of improved company performance; and that the policies, practices and beliefs of those who make the decisions can be just accepted as unimprovable. This even includes the example of banking, which has just failed its collective duty to society almost as completely as the Soviet Union. Going back further, the entire British car industry was destroyed in the 1960s and 1970s by a toxic mix of short-termism, obsession with merger activity and neglect of skills and teamwork. The unions were far from blameless, but the managers escaped with impunity, and a chance for reform was lost. The Thatcher Government quite reasonably introduced trade union and labour market reforms in the 1980s, but did not bother with management reforms, leaving a key cause of economic underperformance untouched.

Ironically, the emphasis by neo-liberals on labour market reform, and the exclusion of management or governance reform, serves to bolster union power, because it hands the unions a permanent grievance. This unbalanced approach has left the actual practice of management, in both the public and private sectors, prey to the cynical and disastrous theories that we discussed in Chapter 3. In so far as there has been 'management reform', it has been negative – a purposeful march away from the evidence base and the principles of sustainability and sound stewardship. Public sector inefficiency in recent years has been caused at least as much by introducing business process re-engineering, agency theory and similar examples of complete nonsense from the Chicago school, as it has by union privileges. But some jurisdictions have managed a spectacular combination of both. Yet there is still little demand for improvement in management practice or theory. We are supposed to put up with bad management, like the weather.

DOES THE ORGANISATION EVEN EXIST?

Business orthodoxy, though it sounds hard-nosed and practical, has actually been based on flaky, abstract principles. They derive in part from accountancy: we have discussed how the concept of 'intangible' assets is really a misnomer: it is the people who exist and the financial accounts that are conceptual. Another main influence is the law. The legal entity that is 'the company' is well defined. In terms of clarifying such important concepts as ownership, liabilities, contractual obligations, financial returns and so on, the invention of the Dutch and English pioneers of the modern concept of 'the company' in the seventeenth century is still serviceable for legal purposes. It is not, however, a definition of the real organisation, and was probably not intended to be. Unfortunately, such an inaccurate concept was used for much of the twentieth century. Leadership and business management have been taught on the basis that 'the company' is a single entity, with a strategy, a model and a set of processes. It could be 're-engineered' or 'leveraged' or 'merged' with another company (these are all inaccurate metaphors, but used so frequently that they pass for description). These familiar terms rest on this fundamentally inaccurate, mono-dimensional concept of what an organisation is – which goes some way to explaining why initiatives based on these metaphors nearly always fail.

This is not how actual organisations are. In everyday working life we never come across a tangible entity that is 'the company'. We deal with relationships. A chief executive of a large corporation cannot possibly know all that occurs in the interactions, deals and conversations of even the senior level of operational managers, never mind the thousands of other staff. He or she spends their day making decisions, talking in meetings or using other communications media.

Tim Casserley of the Edge Equilibrium consultancy, observes:

> *Organisations don't really exist. All that exists is human beings in a constant process; communicating, interacting. I could point you to particular individuals, and to groups moving in the right direction; could I point you to an 'organisation'? I don't think the world works like that. It's much more about coalitions.*

The credit crisis was not caused by individual institutions moving in a certain way as a single entity, but by certain groups of people, motivated by timeless human characteristics such as over-ambition, hubris and miscalculation. Not everyone at the banks that failed made these mistakes; not everyone at the banks that survived were blameless. As noted in Chapter 1, it is essential to avoid the simplistic 'Good Company/Bad Company' stereotype.

This crisis and any other can only be understood in a behavioural context. 'Many people were doing brave things in the run-up to the crisis. Unfortunately, the dominant people were over-blown, grandiose, with ambitions about their own self-aggrandisement', says Mr Casserley.

We agree with Tim that the concept of leadership has to be radically rethought. His observation is absolutely correct that:

> *When senior management decide to go from A to B, with this outcome; it's quite clear that that's a good intention. But to expect that that is exactly what you are going to get is a fantasy of your own making. It relies on other human beings, with their own perspectives.*

This insight applies every bit as much to politics as to corporate leadership. At least in private sector management, there are positive developments towards a better understanding of the unpredictability of human communities and the need for communication to assist certain strategies, and contingency planning in case they do not work. In politics, there remains a more rigid belief that a certain decentralisation, or privatisation, or nationalisation will have predictable, mechanistic outcomes.

He adds:

> *There is a sense of urgency about our mission [for leadership of people, rather than of 'the organisation']; trying to avoid a recurrence of the crisis, which I would see as inevitable. Everyone has gone back to business as usual. I'm very concerned about the legacy. People think it's political, as opposed to philosophical. It's so embedded, the notion that organisations are 'things' that are tangible. It's difficult to get out of that [way of thinking].[1]*

In recent years, there has been growing interest in behavioural finance, and applied psychology in the workplace. The role of cognitive biases, such as illusion of control, groupthink, over-confidence bias, and their influence on decision making, is more widely acknowledged. But in organisational management, there is a barrier before this dimension can be acknowledged: if people think they are dealing with an inanimate object, rather than human beings, psychology is not even admitted entrance. One sees this prejudice on an almost daily basis in many management and board teams where individuals look at the numbers on the Excel sheet and snort derisively at 'the soft stuff'.

---

1   Exclusive interview for this book.

Ultimately, however, people are all you have. It is the people who exist, and 'the organisation' that is the intangible, abstract entity. Get your head around this reorientation and everything becomes clearer. But this leaves huge implications for the way in which we conceive the challenge of leadership. If, as a leader, I am not sitting in the cab of a giant machine, pulling levers, what am I doing?

LEADERSHIP IS PERSONAL

Recasting the leadership challenge as one requiring a high level of people and analytical skills, devoted to the challenge of long-term resilience as well as short-term effectiveness, is profound. Fortunately, there is a wealth of literature and research on this. Indeed, we do not lack research or insight; what has been lacking has been the recognition in political circles and many boardrooms of the importance of leadership development. This has been combined with an over-reliance on restructuring as a way to try to effect change. In the real world, senior leaders within an organisation are not 're-engineering' a discrete entity called 'the organisation'. Instead, they are meeting, negotiating, deciding, motivating, hiring, delegating and communicating. They are dealing with people. The real organisation consists of highly complex network of teams that are rich in human capital. It is more like an organic brain than a single, simplistic entity that can be engineered. Moreover, such complexity, both in organisational arrangements and product and service design, tends to be increasing. This has profound implications at a personal level for the individual leader and manager.

If we reconceive the corporation as a human enterprise, that can benefit commercially from a commitment to sustainability, we can see that leadership style is of central importance, and in crucial dimensions can be very different from those that might have been highly prized in the past. The best leaders are continually learning and developing, and see their abilities at relationship management as being of similar importance to those of business analysis and judgement. There is now a considerable amount of research on the links between a leader's emotional intelligence and the climate within the organisation and commitment of employees, which in turn affects organisational performance. The structure of an organisation is comparatively unimportant.[2] A health warning does have to be sounded here. Some of the work on emotional intelligence has come under criticism, but often from commentators who compare it against a simplistic linear model in which there is supposed to be a simple discrete cause of effective leadership and easily measurable effects. Leadership

---

2   For example, see Goleman, Daniel, McKee, Annie and Boyatzis, Richard, Primal Leadership: The Hidden Driver of Great Performance, *Harvard Business Review*, December 2001; also: Leadership for the 21st Century, Hay Group/LOMA report 1999; also: Mankins, C. and Rogers, R., The Decision-Driven Organization: Forget the Org-chart – the Secret is to Focus on Decisions, not Structure, *Harvard Business Review*, June 2010.

is not like that. Emotionally mature leadership, based on the principles of Daniel Goleman and others, is more likely to nurture employee engagement, which in turn is more likely to generate good results. But success depends also on good judgement and analysis, innovation and, sometimes, luck. There is no silver bullet, and there are no guarantees. Leadership is contextual, and rooted in the real personality. The idea of a set of objectively determined competencies is inaccurate – at best, such concepts are outline indicators. However, the critics of some of the research on emotional intelligence and employee engagement tend to ignore the wider context, especially the baleful influence of negative messages about management from agency theory (see Chapter 3). They complain that emotionally smart leadership and engaged employees are merely necessary, not sufficient, for success, which is true; but its necessary-ness has been disguised or undermined by cynical theories from economic and political ideologies.

Self-awareness is an important check against arrogance or over-ambition in executives. It also should ensure that actions are in line with the values being put forward. For a vivid example of how this can go wrong, you only have to consider the misjudgement of leading automotive executives in the US in 2008 taking personal jets to fly to Washington to formally request Federal bail-out funds. It transpired that the companies had maintained a fleet of jets even while cutting jobs and benefits for their workers. There was political uproar, which ought to have been obvious to someone not caught up in the corporate culture. Of course, the cash saved by selling the fleet would have scarcely made much difference to the losses at the companies; that was not the point. It was the example set; and also the expectation that ordinary employees and taxpayers should subsidise such luxury that caused the political backlash.[3] One could imagine a similar controversy if an avowedly 'green' organisation was flying executives everywhere with a fleet of personal jets.

Because the leadership style needed for the new normal has a heavy behavioural element, it may be that coaching is more suitable than traditional training when developing leaders. Integrity, independence, diversity and ethics are all concepts that cannot easily be 'taught' but rather require individuals to explore their own responses to real events within some structured programme.

There is a balance to be struck in business leadership. The recent rebirth of interest in long-term strategies and sustainability is welcome, but businesses have to be managed in the short term as well. The organisation needs sound cash flow as well as long-term plans. Leaders have to guard against spending too much time on strategy. A valuable tool in making these connections is Ken Wilber's definition of four dimensions of the leader. It is a simple quadrant dividing individual and collective, and interior and exterior. In other words: the individual's interior, such as beliefs;

---

3   Big three CEOs flew private jets to plead for public funds, ABC News, 19 November 2008.

the individual's conduct; the organisation's structures and values; and the external environment.

A mindful leader is a wise steward. He or she has given up the 'command-and-control' approach, but this does not mean retreating into an ivory tower as some sort of guru. It means making the connections between the individual, the team, the organisation and the performance and wider impact. The discussions in earlier chapters about understanding organisations and economies as being essentially behavioural have direct implications for the individual leader.

A FRAMEWORK FOR GOVERNANCE

The notion of a company as a discrete, inanimate entity that can be manipulated or 're-engineered' is a misleading metaphor that has coexisted with the myths, discussed in Chapter 3 (subheading 'Witchcraft, Mesmerism and Agency Theory') that the shareholders 'own' the company and that senior executives are their 'agents'.

There is a further important task that has been obscured by the recent fad of agency theory: the distinction between the roles of directors and of managers. Practical leadership is shared by these roles, but they are distinct. A director of a company is, in nearly all jurisdictions, a stewardship role with legally defined duties towards long-term sustainability, and comes with formidable liabilities for failure to discharge those duties. By contrast, the executives are directly responsible for the day-to-day operational management of the firm, though obviously the most senior play a role in developing strategy. Despite its importance, being a director remains like being an amateur volunteer. There is no automatic requirement for training and qualification, which is remarkable when one considers the level of responsibility entailed, not just for the company but for the state of the wider economy, in the case of the largest firms.

The ideological emphasis in recent decades on market freedom has led to misinterpretation. A free market does not emerge from a complete free-for-all; it requires rules and standards, like a game of sport. We accept this in pharmaceuticals and medicine, where strict controls exist before products can be released for sale or practitioners can practice. In the financial markets, Simon Caulkin has made the excellent suggestion that a new financial product should have to pass regulatory safety tests, like a new drug, before it can be traded. In the case of board directors, surely some threshold has to be reached before individuals assume such weighty responsibilities.

Of course, there have been codes of governance in recent years in many countries, but they have been about structure, not competence, and they have been unduly influenced by the cynical assumptions of agency theory. Recent trends have made a distinction between 'independent' directors and others; and between 'non-executive' and 'executive' directors. According to company law and some long-established principles of governance, these are not the most helpful distinctions. There is a difference between the executive and the director role, but this does not make you 'independent'. The role of director is a contractual duty with the legal entity that is the company, and it is one of long-term stewardship of the company, not day-to-day management. If an executive at the company is also a director and sits on the board, these are two discrete roles. Governance adviser Bob Garratt has recommended that they have two separate contracts: as executive and as director. In the new edition of his classic guide *The Fish Rots from the Head*, he writes: 'Mission-orientated mindsets and behaviours of executives are often in direct opposition to the long-term legal duties of the directors'.[4] A key attribute of the board director is to ask 'intelligently naïve' questions, for example to get under the skin of a technical report from the head of a specialist function. In his experience, few board directors, especially those new to the role, have the confidence to do this.

Developing this idea, one can see how this discipline would have helped avert recent disasters. One can imagine the following intelligently naïve questions being put to certain boards in the recent past:

- *Investment bank board, c. 2005*: 'Should we be trading at all in Securitised Debt Obligations? I can't see what the underlying assets actually are, and therefore what the risk is'.
- *BP, early 2010*: 'Should we be drilling at a depth at which we cannot operate repairs?'.
- *European Union Council of Ministers, early 2000s*: 'Should we press ahead with a single currency for Germany and the likes of Portugal and Greece? They are such different economies'.

These questions could actually be asked by an intelligent child. The risks that they highlight were overlooked in an atmosphere of overconfidence and groupthink.

Garratt has successfully introduced a framework for governance that is radically different from the short-term, opportunistic model of agency theory and shareholder value maximisation. The concept of the 'Learning Board' is particularly enlightened. It removes the common assumption of the omniscience at the senior level, and encourages the concept of a board that is enquiring and responsive; a forum for dissent and debate, as well as the steering group for strategy.

It is no coincidence that Garratt's work with Sir Brian Pitman and the board at Lloyds Bank helped that institution avoid the excessive sub-prime lending and similar high-risk activity – though the institution later became exposed to related liabilities through the merger with Halifax Bank of Scotland.

---

4   Garratt, Bob, *The Fish Rots from the Head*, Revised Edition, Profile Books, 2010.

A board director should be fully inducted and prepared. The board has to set the organisational direction, resist the temptation to interfere or micro-manage; and it needs to act as antennae for the organisation – picking up on external demographic, consumer, political and environmental trends and using this intelligence to inform strategy. The board director should also be committed; Garratt recommends dedicating a day a week to the task – a prospect that 'horrifies' most directors, he says, as they struggle to find time to attend to a monthly meeting and read the papers beforehand. But, he notes:

> *The idea that they will have to do homework and other duties is simply unacceptable. Fine. But they should not then be on the board. This may sound harsh, but the law is clear: once you have signed the statutory requirement to register as a director you are on duty 24 hours a day, seven days a week. You are not a director just when you enter the boardroom or the committee room, or when you are hurriedly reading the board papers.*[5]

CONTROLLING OUR ILLUSIONS

The move away from 'command and control' towards a leadership style of nurturing sustainability, is profound. In recent years, there has been increased awareness, especially in the in the investment community, of the power of cognitive biases, and how even the most intelligent and well informed individuals can be prey. One of the most influential of cognitive biases is: 'illusion of control' – the assumption that it is largely policy-makers and executives who determine what happens in economies and organisations.

The Learning Board, and the Learning Organisation, knows that it certainly cannot predict, and often cannot anticipate, so it has to be responsive, aware and vigilant.

This ought to be a lesson that carries through to politicians, central bankers and the economists who advise them. Too often, they make predictions on the assumption that unexpected events do not occur. They make projections of 'growth' as though they were nurturing a runner bean; as though economies were closed off from such ugly things like earthquakes, weather, drought, political protest or investment bubbles.

The trouble with imagining that we can, or should, control economies or organisations is that on the many occasions that it becomes apparent that we cannot, there is a tendency to flip over into panic mode. Better to acknowledge our limitations, and look at what we are good at. As humans, we overstate our ability to control, and understate our abilities to perceive, and to make relationships. Our best achievements

---

5   Garratt, Bob, *The Fish Rots from the Head*, Revised Edition, Profile Books, 2010.

come from understanding and from cooperation. A human being can perceive an entire galaxy; moreover, astronomers can assess and make some measure of this vast entity. People are also astonishingly adept at communication and cooperation, building and sustaining complex organisations that can extract natural materials, convert them into boats, planes and iPads, and deliver them around the world. Such enterprises do require leadership, and leadership does require decisiveness, but the gifted leaders understand that they cannot command and control everything; nor even know everything that their organisations do.

Organisations that are best able to adapt and retain sufficient autonomy and control are those that invest in communication, engagement and teamwork, rather than an exaggerated idea of the controlling abilities of a central cadre. It is an irony and a paradox, like most useful insights.

INFLATION AND DIVERSIFICATION OF JOB TITLES

Confusion over the actual role and legal responsibilities of a director has coexisted with an explosion of the use of the term 'director' in ordinary and sometimes quite junior management positions (this trend would probably go into reverse if the senior managers and the legal and HR departments woke up to the liabilities incurred by someone formally recognised as a director of a limited company!).

The trend has accompanied a rise in the number of managers in many organisations, especially those in a monitoring role, or sometimes with vaguely defined responsibilities involving the word 'change'. It is difficult to be certain of the causes of these developments. It appears to affect the private sector as well as the public, but perhaps especially the latter. Where previously someone with a modest title like administrator or matron would run a hospital or ward with little fuss or bother, and just the minimum of administrative back-up, now we seem to need an army of auditors, facilitators and change agents, while every other white-collar post is a 'director' of some sort.

The trend is so large and nebulous that it is difficult to be certain about specific causes. In frequent discussions with long-standing managers at many organisations, however, there does seem to be a connection between the frequency of reorganisation and both the growth of management posts and diversity of their titles. Another factor in the public sector is the tendency of politicians to impose performance targets, exacerbating any command-and-control tendencies there may be. This political trend has almost forced some organisations to hire people simply in order to fill in the forms that show the achievement of targets – or in some cases, one suspects, the appearance of reaching targets.

However, the myth of the organisation as a 'machine' manipulated by the CEO (who used to be plain managing director; initials are supposed to sound more executive, trendy and modern) is probably a factor also. Such an individual will have a natural desire to know everything that is going on and to seek to control it. And the frequent reorganisations created by constant desires to 're-engineer' often stir up so much chaos that dozens of new hires are required to get the basic functions working again. This is certainly the case after a merger, where success depends on the dedication of relatively junior individuals who have to work hard to make new teams operate. In some larger organisations, there is a tendency to promote an underperforming manager to a largely functionless office, rather than dismiss them or coach them into a more suitable role. The individual then sometimes seeks to arrange lots of meetings to give the appearance of activity.

The 'machine' metaphor has served to mystify and over-complicate management. Instead of dealing with staff, who need to develop skills and teamwork to serve the customer, guided by a sensible mix of discipline and encouragement, we now seem to be led by metaphors around 're-engineering', 'synergy', 'new paradigms' and other such nonsense. The basic principles of management are comparatively uncomplicated, even if the reality requires considerable reserves of stamina, patience and communication skills. People are complicated and unpredictable enough, without introducing unnecessary complexities.

Another factor is the primacy of PR in a more image-conscious world. If something is not better, it has to be made to sound better. Rebranding occurs in football division titles (in England, the current Division One is actually the third division!); and in school exam results, where there has been an explosion of A grades without any apparent increase in the capability of school leavers. It was inevitable that the trend would apply to managerial job titles, where many a 'director' has far less responsibility than a town clerk or administrator would have wielded in more modest times. The devaluation of the currency is obvious, and it presents real problems.

LEADERSHIP AND MANAGEMENT: DISTINCTIVE BUT LINKED

It is important to make the distinction between governance, leadership and management: the setting of strategy; the execution of strategy and oversight of management; and the day-to-day operations. The unifying element to all, however, is sometimes overlooked: they all concern ways of handling people, and need to be understood in behavioural terms. In the current context, this means moving away from the excessive focus on ownership structures, or metaphors that take the company to be a single entity that can be moulded in a mechanistic way.

There is a wealth of research and literature on all three aspects; what is lacking is not research, but the collective desire to apply this accumulated knowledge. A recent cult of 'maximising shareholder value' has encouraged a focus on managing for short-term results, or even the appearance of good results, and discouraged proper focus on the considerable collective understanding on the principles of sound stewardship of organisations. A further distortion has come from the sectarianism of political thought which has encouraged a tendency to assume that an organisation's capability or ethical stance is determined by whether or not it is a for-profit entity. This reflects a rigid way of viewing politics and organisations according to the left-right perspective. In the next chapter we will argue that this is at best limited, and at worst highly misleading.

CASE STUDY

Westpac – Reform of Governance and Culture towards the Ethic of Sustainability

Background

Westpac is a major Australia-based international bank. It comprises the Westpac Retail and Business Banking (WRBB) with around five million consumer and business customers in Australia under the Westpac and RAMS brands; the Australia-based St George Bank; BT Financial Group, a wealth management branch; Westpac Institutional Bank; and Westpac New Zealand.

It has around 10 million customers in Australia, New Zealand and smaller Pacific islands. It is Australia's oldest bank, having been founded in 1817 as the Bank of New South Wales, changing its name to Westpac in 1982.

Sustainability: A Reaction to Crisis

In the early 1990s, Westpac suffered the largest corporate loss in Australian history. It subsequently embarked upon a downsizing programme that provoked a serious backlash from many communities: over bank branch closures in rural areas and increased charges in particular. Considerable reputational damage was caused by these episodes. Westpac was not alone; there were other corporate failures in Australia in the 1990s. A report commissioned by the bank, and carried out by the Australian Business School, observed:

> During the late 1990s, the chairman, board and executive were under intense media and community pressure, with protests targeted at Westpac by customers, unions and environmental activists. Increased bank fees and branch closures, particularly in rural areas, incensed regional communities. Extensive negative media coverage resulted in a major decline in Westpac's reputational capital and employee morale.[1]

Initial responses that were confined to press relations were ineffective. In the late 1990s the bank's executives embarked on a broader agenda. They sought to reframe the issue as a broader challenge of re-engaging with external stakeholders. Simultaneously,

---

1   Westpac's Squashed Tomato Strategy: Case Study – Sustainable Strategy in Practice at Westpac. Jane Baxter, Wai Fong Chua and Patricia Strong, Australian School of Business, March 2010.

increasing awareness of environmental challenges was growing within the bank's management. These initiatives quickly grew to make sustainable and ethical stewardship an integral part of business strategy.

A background of crisis had a hidden benefit: it meant that the business benefits of managers engaging more with staff and external stakeholders, rebuilding reputation, were more obvious. Tim Williams – Head of Sustainability Strategy at Westpac, says:

> The banks are high-profile companies; shareholders would be pretty disposed to positive action. We had had high-profile corporate failures in the 1990s; there was plenty of value-destruction and there were government inquiries; changes to director duties in corporate law.

A relatively dispersed shareholder ownership and longer-term investment strategies were helpful factors, he adds:

> In Australia there is compulsory superannuation in the pension funds, so there tends to be very wide share ownership, and there are some reasonably progressive pension funds.

Sustainability is Not a Cost to the Business

As Marks & Spencer has also found (see Chapter 4), the business results from enhanced reputation and engagement can be considerable. Tim Williams says:

> From the value generation point of view the proposition is quite compelling; these issues go to the heart of [the matter] … value-generation is a strategic issue. What we have been doing is driving convergence of what would have been a discrete agenda item at one time. It is a drive throughout the business, including the operational business.

In contrast to the conventional financial accounts in the annual report, Westpac's reports now encompass a range of measures. As well as showing the social commitment, they also convey business intelligence.

Implementation of the sustainability strategy has been in three broad areas, according to the analysis by the Australian School of Business:

- engagement with stakeholders;
- public reporting;
- continuous improvement.

On the question of reporting, it is not just a question of public information and transparency. Traditional accounts are historic, and limited to the financial dimension. As discussed in Chapter 1, this cannot encompass such complex matters as risk assessment, human potential and other forward-looking indicators. The People section in the annual report lists indicators such as employee engagement (82 per cent of employees feeling positive about the company's leadership in 2010), proportion of women in senior management (35 per cent). Westpac's reports are as much about informing the business to improve its operations, as they are about demonstrating to the public and to administrators that its conduct is environmentally and socially responsible. The 2010 Australian School of

Business report listed business benefits as: 'Improved staff morale, improved reputational and social capital, both locally and internationally; and a better understanding of the long-term drivers of value creation, profitability and cost savings'. Helping the employer brand considerably has been the succession of awards granted to the bank, including World's Most Ethical Companies, and Employer of Choice for Women. Westpac has been placed in the top 1 per cent of the Governance Metrics International Global Governance Rating.

The reports published by the bank, available on its website are set out in the following table:

Report name	Audience	Comment
Annual report	Investors analysts, shareholders	Financial data
Annual review	Investor groups	Concise annual report
Stakeholder Impact Report	All stakeholders, inc community, employees, customers	Fully accredited sustainability info
PACT newsletter	Employees, customers, suppliers, NGOs, etc	Online newsletter on how Westpac implements sustainability
Extended Performance Reports	Investors, analysts, other interested parties	Half-yearly updates on finance and non-finance indicators

The chief executive and the board take responsibility for the sustainability strategy. The Social Responsibility Committee is at board level.

This approach means that sustainability is likely to remain a core part of Westpac's way of doing business, even if there were an economic downturn that affected the business. It would not be jettisoned as too costly, as it does not represent a cost; moreover it is so tightly woven into both strategic and operational management that it is not a discrete enterprise. Alison Ewings, Senior Adviser Sustainability, comments:

> *It is not a technical function that you can cut; it is a component of our business strategy – it's not something you can put your arms around and say 'We're not going to do it any more'.*

Social Engagement Means Professional Development

Westpac runs educational programmes in all the major countries in which it operates – New Zealand, Australia and the Pacific region. 'On some islands we offer basic help on how the financial system works; much of the population is unbanked', says Alison Ewings.

> *In New Zealand we tie into some of our core business offerings: during the global financial crisis, business customers had to make redundancies, or reduce hours. We helped them with that process, with budgeting tools; helped individuals when they were moving from ten days a fortnight to nine. We have an organisational mentoring programme. We have engaged in capacity-building: working with existing partners, traditional relationships. We also helped indigenous communities, social enterprises: our employees will work*

with those organisations for a couple of years, one day a week – it is formally part of their professional development programme. There are performance discussions and personal development discussions with their manager.

The bank also works with charitable organisations. One of the most effective ways of doing this is to lend its corporate expertise to help with specialist needs of certain departments within the charity. One example was for a charity specialising in research on child diabetes. They had a problem with retention of staff. Secondment of analysts from Westpac's human resources department helped the agency devise diagnostics and systems that reduced the staff turnover rate from 40 per cent to 10 per cent. It often helps NGOs put in effective financial controls.

There are some advantages that come back to Westpac from such initiatives, Ms Ewings reports.

These [secondments] tend to be for employees who are identified as high performers – they might not otherwise get experience of an end-to-end project.

Some 455 of the bank's employees have contributed approximately 72 years in voluntary work with the Jawun Indigenous Corporate Partnerships, primarily by sharing skills with businesses run by indigenous people, and extending financial education to individuals and families.

IN SUMMARY

It is absurd that, while policy-makers and the economists who influence them often call for labour market reform, there is almost never a call for leadership and management reform. This is despite empirical evidence that industrial leadership plays a major, and probably the major, contribution in building successful economies. It helps to redefine leadership in terms of an understanding of the role of all different stakeholders as part of an interdependent enterprise. This also helps with the increasing demand to be sustainable in environmental terms.

FURTHER READING

Governance

Garratt, Bob, *The Fish Rots from the Head: The Crisis in our Boardrooms – Developing the Crucial Skills of the Competent Director*, Profile Books, New Edition, 2010.

Pearson, Gordon, *The Road to Cooperation: Escaping the Bottom Line*, Gower Publishing, 2012.

Personal Leadership

Whiteley, Philip and Bloch, Susan, *Complete Leadership*, Pearson, 2003.

Casserley, Tim and Megginson, David, *Learning from Burnout*, Butterworth Heinemann, 2008.

Wilber, Ken, *A Theory of Everything: An Integral Vision for Business, Politics, Science and Spirituality*, Gateway, 2001.

CHAPTER 6

BEYOND LEFT AND RIGHT

In the old normal, it was assumed that 'progressive' campaigning – based on a notion of building a better, fairer society and protecting the environment – was primarily an activity of the non-profit sector: voluntary organisations, trade unions, some government agencies, and so on. Private business concerned itself only with profit – and often profit at any cost. In the new normal, progressive leadership can come from anywhere. Profit 'at any cost' is not a viable option, because society and the environment can no longer bear those costs, and often an individual business cannot either. Sustainability has become a core business discipline; commodity price risks, for example, are of direct concern to insurers and the finance department. We have to learn to be more cooperative, less partisan.

What has always been hidden from view in conventional ways of viewing economics and business has been the high degree of cooperation and trust required to make organisations work. Conventional political philosophies assume a mutual competition or even hostility between constituencies. Now, competition does exist, but it isn't the whole story. If it was, there would be no corporate successes in the mutual sector; organisations like Whole Foods, John Lewis and Nationwide Building Society simply would not survive. The fact that they do, and can be regarded as top performers, with high levels of profits and impressive long-term resilience, indicates that we have systematically understated the centrality of cooperation and trust. This is the biggest, simplest and most damaging error of agency theory: the pretence that the interests of different stakeholders *never* overlap, as though it were in the interest of a CEO for the business to fail; prompting elaborate arrangements of treats and punishments as though the executives were rats and the business a maze.

When you interview a successful entrepreneur, or chief executive of a more traditional company, they will talk as much about engagement, inspiration and teamwork, as they do about the work ethic, controlling costs and outsmarting the competition. There is no simple formula. The interests of employees, stockholders, executives and the environment are not the *same*; but there is an overlap, and a mutual dependence. Good negotiation skills do not mean annihilating a different constituency, in the old style of industrial relations; nor trying to manipulate them, under agency theory. It means asserting your interests, but also identifying common ground, and exercising enlightened self-interest when you have a long-term interest in maintaining the viability of another stakeholder.

This is now well established in research studies that go back decades. A summary of suggested reports and books is listed at the end of Chapter 3. They have never been taken seriously because the beliefs of dominant political philosophies were so deeply ingrained that their adherents were not looking in the right place for evidence; or, more typically, were not looking for evidence at all. The events of 1989 buried one set of myths but led to a resurgence of others, as discussed in Chapter 3. Belief in the zero-sum game – in which every 'gain' for the worker is supposed to represent an equally and opposite loss for the owner or manager, continued.

You see this in debates over employee rights legislation, especially in Europe. The trade unions assume that every additional right is a gain for the worker; the employers' groups argue that it is always an additional cost to the business. Both assume a simplistic 'zero-sum' relationship is at work, rather than the realities of a complex interrelationship, with some overlaps of interest. In the real world, it is possible that new employee rights legislation does not help workers have more job security or higher wages, but it is also possible that they can help the business, rather than be a 'cost'. It depends on the context, and what the worker offers in return for the enhanced pay or reduced hours, or right to equal treatment. Both sides ignore the needs of the other side, and would presumably fear a backlash within their own communities if they were to acknowledge that the other 'side' had legitimate claims. As we saw in the example of Marks & Spencer's programme to increase wages in Bangladesh, when such an initiative is handled in an intelligent way both 'sides' benefit. What matters most with a pay rise is how it is effected, and what is offered in return. This is the route to making it sustainable.

The revelation that employee relations is not a zero-sum game, or always a case of competition, has profound implications that extend well beyond the MBA classroom. It transforms everything in economics and politics. This includes the very notion of what constitutes a progressive view, if your aims are to overcome discrimination, poverty and ecological degradation. It also transforms our understanding of commerce, if your aim is to create successful organisations. Moreover, it opens up the exciting possibility of addressing both agendas simultaneously, as the case studies in this book illustrate. The findings also place a question mark over the 'left' versus 'right' perspectives, which we argue have conventionally been based on the flawed operating assumption that the interests of business owners and workers are mutually opposed.

The findings on management, organisational design and employee engagement, from Elton Mayo in the 1930s to Professor Jeffrey Pfeffer today, are the equivalent to management, politics and economics of the great breakthroughs of Galileo, Isaac Newton and Michael Faraday to the physical sciences. This applied anthropology from the human relations school has yielded tremendous insights that can inform the stewardship of our great institutions and economies. It can only be opposed by clinging to the non-sequitur that underlies conventional economics, which is that economies and organisations do not consist of people; or at best that they consist of simplistic, acquisitive machine-like people.

The very terms of reference need to change. Just as the economic collapse of Marxism in 1989 opened up opportunities for change, so does the equivalent collapse of Friedmanism in 2008. What is less obvious is that the challenge for the left is every bit as daunting as that of the right. In our experience, many institutions of the left are captured or heavily influenced by Friedmanism and its cynical assumptions, as we shall set out to demonstrate.

In the old normal, economics was money and employee relations was war. In the new normal, economics is people and employee relations is communication. This is not a softer alternative, because people can be difficult and communication can be fraught. It is a more realistic one.

One of the most baleful consequences of looking at the world through the 'left/ right' prism is the refusal to explore how wealth is created, and instead fall back on simplistic binary alternatives around monetary theory. The sterile debates surrounding different forms of economic stimuli, that may or may not help the west out of its post-credit crunch malaise, are rooted in the old normal, and lack crucial dimensions. From the left it is assumed that all public spending is a 'stimulus', and there is a tendency to defer deficit reduction indefinitely; from the right there is an assumption that the state is always a drag on productive capacity. The paucity of options preferred is an embarrassment; the crucial elements that are overlooked are glaring – if you actually stop to consider where and how wealth is generated in an economy. The terms of reference in the shallow and tedious debates currently raging in western political capitals concern the quantum of money manipulated, not the way in which it is spent – an aspect which might include an assessment of impact on future earning potential. This debate is overlaid on the traditional left/ right tussle over the size of the state. Instead of the binary delusion of the Keynesian versus neo-liberal debate, the focus ought to be placed on the *quality* of public and private investments, and the nurturing of specialist business clusters. As an example, Rolls Royce recently announced an audit showing the wider economic benefit of a hi-tech, successful export company to an economy. This type of analysis leads to the kind of understanding that ought to lie at the heart of politicians' deliberations. There has to be recognition that both the public sector and the private sector can be wasteful: the former typically through lack of accountability and cronyism; the latter in misallocations of capital such as investment bubbles.

There is a need for a departure from the centuries-old turf wars of left and right, to look more forensically at the needs of a modern economy and society. The contours of a post-left/right debate would feature the following considerations:

- Sustainability is for governments and trade unions, as well as corporations.
- Follow the money, look at vested interests.
- Change tactics, not principles, as the context alters.
- What is the progressive agenda, and where does progressive leadership come from?
- How can political leaders confront contemporary challenges?

We shall address each of these challenges in turn.

SUSTAINABILITY IS FOR THE LEFT, TOO – DEBT IS NOT PROGRESSIVE

Aggregate sovereign debt in the western countries is now measured in the trillions of dollars. In part, this reflects the scale of the bail-outs of the banking industry. It is also the result, however, of spending on social programmes. Some governments, such as those in Germany, the UK, the USA and Italy, were running significant deficits before the banking bail-outs, and despite years of economic growth. This is now a dangerous situation, especially as, by some analyses, the era of cheap capital may be ending, meaning that the costs of running high deficits are almost certain to rise, and they may become unaffordable.[1] Political parties that pride themselves on public spending programmes are reluctant to accept that the government deficits and house-price booms of recent years can have regressive impacts – transferring wealth from younger, low-income people to older people with property.

In the new normal, public spending cannot be automatically exempted from the economics of sustainability. Government borrowing, unless it raises the long-term productive capacity of the nation – something rarely prioritised in party political manifestos – can end up as simply a tax on the young. Waste in public spending encourages waste of natural resources, because wasteful practices are behavioural and infectious.

At the time of writing, there is heavy emphasis by centre-left parties in the west on a tactic of deficit-spending to create a 'stimulus' to prevent a 'double-dip' recession. The potential for government borrowing to achieve this alchemy is exaggerated, and the policy involves long-term risk. If economic activity is very subdued, and borrowing is low, there is a case for government borrowing to stimulate some kind of recovery; to kick the patient into some kind of life, akin to a medical team applying electrical shocks to the heart. In practice, however, many western governments have begun to depend upon this 'stimulus' on an ongoing basis. The most obvious example was Greece, where ministers simply treated borrowed cash is if it were

---

1   Dobbs, Richard and Spence, Michael, The Era of Cheap Capital Draws to a Close, *McKinsey Quarterly*, February 2011.

income, like a credit card delinquent, but the practice has spread, even to the USA, with its quantitative easing, eye-wateringly high deficits, and political paralysis that inhibits efforts to curb the borrowing. In January 2011 the Congressman John Campbell observed: 'We are much closer to the Greece–Ireland–Spain precipice than any of us would like to believe'.

Public spending is often rebranded 'investment' to make it sound less wasteful. Sometimes, it can properly be regarded as such. Market fundamentalists are wrong to assume that all public spending is a drag on the economy, especially given the central role of education, and in particular research universities, in economic development. Advanced economies feature high levels of cooperation between the public and private sector, especially on investment in human capital (see further reading at the end of this chapter). But if politicians want their spending programmes to be regarded as investment, they have to accept the disciplines of investment, and demonstrate a return. This is not hypothetical: Nehru's investment in the Indian Technology Colleges in the 1950s have returned their cost many thousands of times over in the succeeding decades, and was probably the single most important factor in converting India from an underdeveloped nation to an economic power.

Too often, however, borrowing is used for revenue spending, not investment. Across the west, we have become so accustomed to easy credit facilities that the dangers of high debt are obscured. The eyes are always on the next GDP figures. As Congressman Campbell made his sobering warning, the most recent 'growth' figures for the USA (we put the term in inverted commas because high borrowing can often just produce the illusion of growth) showed an increase to 3.2 per cent on an annual basis. This prompted expressions of relief around the west, even though the underlying debts were growing. Debts at state level are beginning to assume gigantic proportions. Joshua Rauh, an economist at Northwestern University, has calculated that underfunded liabilities had reached around $3 trillion by the end of 2008. The state of Illinois is due to run out of money to pay pensions by 2018, Rauh calculates, using a generous assumption of 8 per cent asset returns. Connecticut, New Jersey and Indiana face the crunch in 2019.[2] The bankrupt states will presumably expect a federal bail-out, but the end of the current decade is just the point at which the federal government itself is likely to hit crunch point, unless there is a dramatic turnaround in Washington politics, and a concerted effort to reduce the deficit in the few years between now and then. But not to worry, annual GDP growth at the end of 2010 was 3.2 per cent! So all is well!

---

2   Are State Public Pensions Sustainable? Why the Federal Government Should Worry About State Pension Liabilities. Joshua Rauh, Northwestern University, Paper for the National Bureau of Economic Research, 15 May 2010. Cited in Tett, Gillian, Outlook for munis heralds arbitrage opportunities, *Financial Times*, 10 February 2011.

At the time of writing, the US trade deficit had increased to $500 billion, from $370 billion in 2009. The final budget deficit figure for 2010 was on course to be $1.5 trillion, over 10 per cent of GDP.[3] It is anticipated that total debt will reach 100 per cent of GDP by the end of the decade. It is a similar story in the European Union (EU), where the theoretical 'ceilings' of deficits of 3 per cent of GDP and 60 per cent of debt were broken years ago and have spiralled further upwards following the bank rescues. Inflation and default are likely to be the only long-term options for the west, and they bring with them serious problems of reduced relative living standards.

In the USA and the EU we have been living beyond our means for many years now, which would not be a serious problem if we acknowledged it. Instead, euphemisms have crept in to support deficit spending and associated investment bubbles. House price inflation becomes 'recovery'; government borrowing is called a 'stimulus', while reducing that borrowing is referred to as 'austerity measures'. Plus becomes minus and minus becomes plus. Sloppy or dishonest use of vocabulary leads to equally unreliable arithmetic.

It is true that a very sharp reduction in government spending can have a destabilising effect, but this does not automatically make high levels of borrowing safe. There are no easy solutions, but that is a measure of the extent of policy errors by governments and banks over the past decade or so.

FOLLOW THE MONEY

In the conventional analysis, investment bank activity is seen as 'right wing' and social spending by the state as 'left wing', but behaviourally there are certain similarities between centre-left governments and the banks – especially with regards to over-optimism and a mutual interest in government spending programmes. In recent years some penetrating analyses from the finance community have exposed how, ironically, left-wing governments have helped to create short-term profits for investment banks, while creating a future debt-repayment problem for their populations.

Among those exposing these dynamics, worthy of particular mention are Jason Manolopoulos, Walter Molano and Simon Johnson, the first two from the investment community, the last a former IMF executive. They have produced some valuable reports on the oligarchical nature of the investment banks and how, for all the rhetorical opposition, the labour parties of Europe and the Democrats in the US have bolstered their activities and profits. Profligate western governments, usually though not always formally 'left wing', are some of Goldman Sachs' most profitable

---

3   See http://www.usgovernmentspending.com/federal_deficit_chart.html [accessed 28 October 2012].

customers, because they borrow so much. In one notorious case, the Wall Street institution colluded with Greek socialist ministers effectively to defraud future taxpayers on a huge scale.

Jason Manolopoulos observes in his chronicle of the eurozone crisis, *Greece's Odious Debt*:

> As details emerged, it transpired that more investment banks, and more Governments, were involved in the deception. As in the North American sub-prime crisis, use of financial derivatives played a role in disguising the extent and riskiness of debt – in this case European sovereign debt.

In an observation that renders as useless the distinctions between 'left' and 'right', and between social democratic Europe and free-market USA, Manolopoulos adds that a mountain of sovereign debt was built up over several years, with short-termist politicians and investment bankers profiting equally. It permitted the peripheral nations of the eurozone to accumulate too much hard-currency debt for such small economies.[4]

Experienced Argentina-watcher Walter Molano, head of research at BCP Securities, said in 1999:

> Why was the [Wall] Street so positive on Argentina a year ago, when the Menem Government was the picture of complacency? Why did the Street forgive all of Argentina's excessive borrowing between 1997 and 1999? Why did the Street ignore Argentina's lack of fiscal discipline during the past four years? It probably has nothing to do with the fact that Argentina was one of the biggest bond issuers in the world during that same period.[5]

In February 2010, *The New York Times* disclosed that:

> Instruments developed by Goldman Sachs, JP Morgan Chase and other banks enabled politicians to mask additional borrowing in Greece, Italy and possibly elsewhere.

This article also revealed how Goldman Sachs, in late 2009, discussed with ministers of the ruling Greek socialist PASOK Government, setting up a financing instrument that 'would have pushed debt from Greece's health care system far into the future'.[6]

---

4   Manolopoulos, Jason, *Greece's Odious Debt*, Anthem Finance, 2011. As a declaration of interest, Philip Whiteley helped with research for this book.
5   Latin American Adviser, 15 December 2000, also quoted in Blustein, Paul, *And the Money Kept Rolling In (and Out)*, Perseus Books, 2005.
6   Wall St helped to mask debt fueling Europe's crisis, *New York Times*, 13 February 2010.

The currency swap arranged between Greek ministers of the socialist PASOK Government and Goldman Sachs in 2001–2002 was mutually beneficial to ministers in disguising the total debt in preparation for entry into the single currency, and was profitable for Goldman Sachs for the fees it received for arranging the complex transaction. But it had the effect of increasing the longer-term borrowing costs – a cost that falls upon the taxpayer. Some details of the currency swap featured in *Risk Magazine* two years later, but it complained that both the Greek Government and Goldman Sachs declined to comment, and that key details were kept secret – an extraordinary state of affairs considering this concerned taxpayers' money in a European democracy: an investment bank and a government treating other people's money as a confidential matter! The arrogance is breathtaking. The magazine reported:

> *The cross-currency swaps transacted by Goldman for Greece's public debt division were 'off-market' – the spot exchange rate was not used for re-denominating the notional of the foreign currency debt. Instead, a weaker level of euro versus dollar or yen was used in the contracts, resulting in a mismatch between the domestic and foreign currency swap notionals. The effect of this was to create an upfront payment by Goldman to Greece at inception, and an increased stream of interest payments to Greece during the lifetime of the swap. Goldman would recoup these non-standard cashflows at maturity, receiving a large 'balloon' cash payment from Greece.*

The *Risk* article added that the fee paid to Goldman Sachs for the arrangement 'was approximately $200 million'. Sadly, taxpayers do not benefit from consumer protection legislation.

What is extraordinary about these scandals is just how little coverage they have received in Europe. As European taxpayers, we have to read the *New York Times*, or specialist financial papers, for some of the most telling details on how we have been deceived. Also worthy of recognition is the Italian economist Gustavo Piga, who uncovered much of the deficit-manipulation in Europe.[7] The 2001–2002 Greek currency swap affected every taxpayer in Europe as it helped Greece enter the single currency. It is now widely acknowledge that the Greek economy was in no fit state to enter the euro, and the mounting costs of the rescue are affecting the entire continent.

Controversies over high levels of government borrowing, and use of derivatives to push debt costs further into the future, are more or less ignored by mainstream media. Few western politicians face tough questioning on the matter – indeed, it is those trying to rein in high borrowing who receive the toughest grilling as they defend their 'austerity' measures. There is an institutional bias towards debt. This

---

7   See, for example, Eurostat rules described 'Greek-type' swap, *Risk Magazine*, 18 February 2010.

creates a moral hazard: there is now a significant incentive for a president or prime minister to increase spending and borrowing in the run-up to an election that they fear they may lose, safe in the knowledge that a successor will take the blame for the consequences.

There is also a shared lexicon between the left and the investment banking community. Take, for example, the following quote, from Jan Hatzius, chief US economist for Goldman Sachs, interviewed on the *Financial Times* podcast in February 2011. The word 'stimulus' is used for spending programmes that depend heavily upon borrowing; the word 'drag' is used for curbing such borrowing:

> *We do think that state and local government spending is going to be one of the weaker parts: definitely one of the lagging sectors. State and local government probably subtracted half a percentage point from growth in 2010, via a combination of tax increases and spending cuts, and I think the impact is still going to be negative in 2011; maybe not quite as large, but still negative. In terms of the money coming from federal government to the state governments, that's obviously drying up in 2011. It is still going to be a drag.*[8]

You could remove the title 'chief US economist, Goldman Sachs' and insert the name and job title of pretty much any centre-left politician from the west, and no one would notice the difference.

It works the other way around. When the then UK Chancellor Gordon Brown opened the new London office of Lehman Brothers in 2004, he declared:

> *I would like to pay tribute to the contribution you and your company make to the prosperity of Britain. During its 150-year history, Lehman Brothers has always been an innovator, financing new ideas and inventions before many others even began to realise their potential.*

Many of the 'new ideas' developed by the investment banking industry in that period did indeed 'realise their potential' by the end of the decade, though not exactly in the way that the speaker envisaged. Six years later, the plaque commemorating Gordon Brown's opening was sold at an auction by PricewaterhouseCoopers, Lehman Brothers' administrator after its liquidation. It fetched £28,750.

Simon Johnson, formerly of the IMF, directly accuses the investment bank community of 'capturing' major governments of right, left and centre in the west. The right-wing parties have bought into the deregulation agenda, while the left enjoy the easy borrowing arrangements to fund social programmes.

---

8   Goldman: US recovery is sustainable, podcast broadcast, ft.com, 10 February 2011.

In the US, while the left-wing blame deregulation for the credit crisis, and the right-wing blame the Clinton administration's encouragement of home-ownership in lower-income groups, Johnson identifies a common factor: 'Even though some [policies] are traditionally associated with Democrats and some with Republicans, they *all* benefited the financial sector'.

Some of the repeals encouraged by the investment banks have been:

- insistence on free movement of capital across borders;
- repeal of Depression-era regulations separating commercial and investment banking;
- congressional ban on the regulation of credit-default swaps;
- major increases in the amount of leverage allowed to investment banks;
- light hand at the Securities and Exchange Commission in regulatory enforcement;
- international agreement to allow banks to measure their own riskiness;
- an 'intentional' failure to update regulations so as to keep up with the tremendous pace of financial innovation.

With experience in financial crises in emerging markets, Johnson has identified a similar pattern in the 'advanced' economies, with the large investment banks behaving like oligarchs.

> *In its depth and suddenness, the US economic and financial crisis is shockingly reminiscent of moments we have recently seen in emerging markets (and only in emerging markets): South Korea (1997), Malaysia (1998), Russia and Argentina (time and again).*[9]

In February 2011 he renewed his criticism, writing of the hypocrisy of the banks in emphasising the importance of reducing sovereign debt, given that their reckless behaviour, in concert with politicians, was responsible for so much of it:

> *No one forced the banks to take on so much risk. Top bankers lobbied long and hard for the rules that allowed them to behave recklessly. Politicians should call the bluff of bankers who 'threaten' to move to a different jurisdiction: The idea that megabanks would move to other countries is simply ludicrous. These behemoths need a public balance sheet to back them up, or they will not be able to borrow anywhere near their current amounts.*[10]

---

9   The Quiet Coup, Simon Johnson, *Atlantic* Magazine, May 2009.

10   Johnson, Simon, The ruinous fiscal impact of big banks, *New York Times* Economix blog, 3 February 2011.

He notes the incestuous relationship between investment banks and the US Treasury, with senior personnel often moving from one to the other, muddying the waters between an industry and the institution that is supposed to police it. There has been a similar pattern in Europe. The Taioseach of Ireland, Brian Cowen, for example, had dinner and played golf with Sean Fitzpatrick, the chairman of Anglo Irish Bank, shortly before passing on to Irish taxpayers the full costs of the ruinously high aggregate debts built up by Anglo Irish and other banks. He declared that business was not discussed at the meeting. Did it need to be?

Much of the content of this book is optimistic, emphasising the potential for partnership across sectors. But dispensing with the 'left/right' prism also helps put a focus on vested interests rather than ownership structure. In this way, you are better equipped to follow the money and uncover malpractice. Hiding behind the shield of the 'left/right' definition feeds a lazy sectarianism in which all the bad things are dumped onto one sector or another, disguising the actual exploitative (or enlightened) behaviour that might emerge in either. Just as the cynical assumptions of right-wing and left-wing orthodoxy hide from us the possibilities of enlightened leadership and its transformative effect upon society, they can also disguise from us the realities of the workings of vested interests.

WAS IT ALL THE BANKS' FAULT?

The political narrative that has now gained ground in the west, especially in Europe, is that the colossal level of sovereign debt is entirely the fault of excesses by the banks and the consequent bail-outs, and that borrowing for social programmes, or unaffordable pensions schemes, were not contributory factors. This is probably a fair summary for Iceland and Ireland. Elsewhere, it does not pass scrutiny. Italy, Belgium and Greece should never have been allowed into the single currency, as they did not meet the criteria on deficits and debts; eurozone governments then used the cheaper borrowing facilities of the new currency to pile up more debt. Gerhard Schroeder's Social Democrat Government in Germany was in flagrant breach of the convergence criteria in 2003, but insouciantly defied the EU's leaders to issue a sanction, and they backed down. Gordon Brown in the UK was repeatedly warned about high levels of risky lending in the UK, the illusion of 'growth' built on too much debt and the systemic risk that it posed. He dismissed such warnings, often contemptuously. He began deficit spending before the banking crash; running a deficit in 2007 after 15 years of continued economic growth. He responded by declaring 'no more boom and bust', claiming to have unilaterally abolished the economic cycle.

In the amnesiac culture of the 24-7 news culture, even last's year's news is ancient history, so these errors of hubris and excessive borrowing by Brown, Schroeder et al. a few years ago are forgotten. It is very difficult to plan for the long term when the culture of news reporting and political discourse refuses to accept that the long term even exists.

As for the US, the deficit has been building for so long, under both Republican and Democrat Governments, that most politicians seem to have forgotten that debt involves borrowing and that borrowing involves interest payments and credit risk. One economist, James Galbraith, perhaps forgivably hubristic given his famous surname, even put forward the interesting idea that the risks of deficit spending – by implication, at any level – are zero. His actual words were:

> The danger [of the long-term deficit] is zero. It's not overstated. It's completely misstated.

He explained:

> The government needs to run a deficit, it's the only way to inject financial resources into the economy.

Like Mr Hatzius of Goldman Sachs and the left-wing governments of Europe, he keeps getting his plus and minus signs mixed up.

Mr Galbraith, whose job title is 'economist and the Lloyd M. Bentsen Jr. chair in government and business relations at the University of Texas', feels the need to explain to those of us who have not benefited from academic study in economics how it works:

> What people worry about is that the federal government won't be able to sell bonds. But there can never be a problem for the federal government selling bonds. It goes the other way. The government's spending creates the bank's demand for bonds, because they want a higher return on the money that the government is putting into the economy. My father said this process is so simple that the mind recoils from it.[11]

The point at which no one wants those bonds anymore, because they fear they will not get their money back, is sufficiently far into the future that Mr Galbraith may not have to worry about it. Generations of future Galbraiths may have a rather different perspective.

Paul Blustein, author of a book on the Argentine default and economic crash of 2001 offered an alternative hypothesis: 'It could happen here. Americans who give Argentina's story fair consideration and conclude otherwise are deluding

---

11   Galbraith: The danger posed by the deficit 'is zero'. Interview with Ezra Klein, *Washington Post*, 12 May 2010.

themselves'.[12] He wrote this in 2005, when the budget deficit was $413 billion. It has since tripled.

CHANGE TACTICS, NOT PRINCIPLES

Looking through the conventional left/right prism, the governments of Europe, including centre-left ones, and the investment bank community, appear at opposite ends of a spectrum. Viewed behaviourally, however, they have been close. The common points have been irrational exuberance, short-termism and a shared delight in eye-wateringly high levels of government borrowing. 'Debt is good' is the shared mantra. It means bumper profits for the banks, and votes for the politician. Their instinct is: The victims are in the future and we will have retired by then.

Increasingly in the west, left-wing movements turn to the banks and to the government for economic growth, or the illusion of growth, rather than to industry and invention. They are uninterested in business and how sustainable wealth is actually created.

Instead of focusing on the distinctions between public and private sector or left versus right, which are superficial, we encourage more focus on vested interests versus fair dealings. With this perspective, some investment banks and more militant public sector unions resemble one another, as 'rent-seekers'. Rent-seeking is defined as when an individual, organisation or firm seeks to gain a premium over a fair income through monopoly or political favour, rather than by earning profits through economic transactions and the production of added wealth. Thomas Philippon of New York University and Ariell Reshef of the University of Virginia have estimated that between 30 per cent to 50 per cent of the extra pay that bankers receive, in comparison to similar professionals, is attributable to 'renting'.[13] In a similar way, it is unusual for trade unions in the public sector to volunteer productivity improvements in return for the pay rises, better pensions, increased legislative working rights or job security that they ask of politicians.

A weakness in conventional left-wing approaches has been an undue focus upon entitlement. Every time a European government proposes a change that does not directly benefit the public sector workforce, there is immediate and unyielding opposition, even where this concerns, for example, a modest increase in the retirement age, far lower than a recent increase in longevity. The dominant narrative is based around the concept of entitlement. This can become rent-seeking behaviour, as it is a one-sided demand – unless there is equal commitment to helping the productive economy, and very few individuals on the left are aware of this danger. The conduct

---

12   Blustein, Paul, *And the Money Kept Rolling In (and Out)*, Perseus Books, 2005.
13   See http://people.virginia.edu/~ar7kf/papers/pr_rev15_submitted.pdf [accessed 28 October 2012]. See also Manolopoulos, Jason, *Greece's Odious Debt*, Anthem Finance, 2011.

may be less aggressive than the rent-seeking behaviour of some investment banks, but the danger it poses is real.

There is unsufficient critique of the tactics of trade unions in the light of a very changed context of long life expectancy, high levels of employment protection and high government deficits. This makes it difficult for unions to renew and modernise. There are times when demands by trade unions for new entitlements from a government or corporation are absolutely justifiable in the context of confronting an exploitative or unreasonable power. But this is less common these days; often they are dealing with well-intentioned institutions trying to contain spiralling costs. In this context, it is more progressive to seek partnership. In the old normal, partnership with business leaders was ruled out as capitulation or 'selling out'; but those conditions do not always apply. In some notable examples, leadership of the progressive agenda is being taken up by the business community. The trade union Prospect has picked up this agenda and worked with enlightened business leaders, doing far more to lift people out of poverty than a confrontational approach could possibly achieve.

In the case of retirement plans, for example, these have to be affordable. Given that life expectancy in the west has risen not just by a few years, but by a couple of decades since the mid-twentieth century, there has to be some movement. If pension arrangements and retirement ages are to be unaltered, or diminished only slightly, what can the trade union movement do to boost the productive economy to ensure that these entitlements are affordable? It is all very well calling for higher taxes, but there has to be a sufficiently substantial productive base in place to be taxed. Otherwise, the entire economy is locked into a downward spiral towards poverty. This is a leadership duty every bit as much for the left as well as for the right. Indeed, it is remarkable that some business groups, traditionally opposed to workplace regulation, actually have resisted ending the compulsory retirement age, upon the ageist notion that individuals over 65 are functionally useless. Both left and right have to begin to acknowledge the reality of longer life expectancy, to see it as an opportunity, but also to ensure that the economics remain viable.

The left is more loyal to its tactics than to its principles. In the early days of the trade union and labour movement, it was logical to lobby for laws to compel industrialists to treat the workers better, and for higher wealth taxes to fund hospitals and social security. In a context of shockingly low wages and job security, and patchy social care, this was broadly acceptable to anyone who wanted to alleviate poverty. Yet it does not follow that, in a very different context, every extra tax and every extra regulation enhances the ability of working people to move out of poverty or avoid discrimination. As discussed in previous chapters, it is now well established that exploiting workers does not add to profits, and this is increasingly being accepted by business leaders – not at the pace that we would like, but the message is reaching that constituency faster than it is being accepted by trade union leaders. Compelling a business owner by law to pay more or behave differently sends out the clear message that it must be against the commercial interest to do so. In this way, the conventional left buys into the neo-liberal theory that sweating the workers harder always add to profits. It is an irony, but one of the few remaining redoubts of undiluted Friedmanism is in the leadership of trade unions, especially the more militant and vocal representatives that attract much airplay in the UK, Spain and Greece. Of course, trade unionists argue that exploiting the workers for more profit is a bad thing, where Friedman would have argued it was a good thing – but both sides are united on the ideological point. And both are fundamentally wrong. Moderate trade unionists often temper this view, depending on the audience, but it still has a tendency to creep in. A few years ago John Monks, then the head of the TUC in the UK, gave a talk at the Work Foundation in which he urged business leaders not to be afraid of workplace recognition rules, citing evidence that organisations that consult with their staff tend to be more successful. But a few minutes later he urged that such rules be made both international and strictly enforced to prevent business leaders 'social dumping' – that is, gaining competitive advantage by evading the law! It is impossible to know which of the two diametrically opposed views he believes in. We hold to the former; but doing so implies profound changes for the beliefs and tactics of trade unions, something that only a few in the movement have recognised.

In any case, it is simply impractical for the law to rule on every workplace relationship, monitor every appointment and socially engineer a harmonious or more equal workplace. The quest would result in byzantine bureaucracy almost certain to increase inequality and create perverse incentives, because it rests on a warped understanding of human nature: the stereotyped generalisation that all 'workers' are oppressed and all bosses manipulative and cynical. In this way, left-wing orthodoxy is remarkably similar to the neo-liberal fad of agency theory (see Chapter 4), which simply rules out the possibility of an enlightened, emotionally intelligent leadership.

This section may appear to be heavily critical of the left, but we are seeking to highlight certain similarities with the right, and above all to encourage an analysis based on behaviour, rather than assume that formal ideology or ownership structure determines everything. So ingrained is the binary delusion, however, that it is simply assumed that a criticism of the left is a defence of the right, and vice versa. Real politics does not contain itself to this narrow, two-dimensional spectrum. The unchanged narrative: that the non-profit sector is in the vanguard of bringing about a fairer society, confronting the exploitative instincts of the for-profit sector, has begun seriously to clash with reality. The reality is that exploitation is behavioural, not the product of imaginary historical or market 'forces', nor the sole preserve of a sector of the economy defined by ownership structure. It is equally possible that the public sector exploits the private sector, as vice versa.

WHAT IS A 'PROGRESSIVE' AGENDA?

In the old normal, the test of whether you were 'progressive', in working towards a fairer society, or overcoming poverty or discrimination, was usually determined by sector – by being in the protest movement, a trade union or the welfare arm of the public sector. In conventional political terms of reference this would be described as left-wing. What we have found in our work, and in the research for this book, is that these distinctions, which were never wholly accurate, are increasingly unreliable – indeed, almost meaningless in some contexts.

If you talk to the employees and above all the customers of organisations, they will describe human and cultural factors, rather than the constitutional framework when asked to describe the moral framework: the service they received, the boss they worked for, perhaps adding conspiratorially a nugget of 'secret' information telling you the inside story. It is human behaviour that determines the conduct of institutions and the experience of those they exist to serve. All organisations are complex networks of human communities that are constantly changing. The purpose here is to warn against sectarianism – that is, making generalised hate figures of those in one sector or another. We would caution against using impersonal metaphorical terms such as 'Big Oil' or 'Big Pharma' – typically used with a pejorative tone, perhaps in a sarcastic manner – to describe a diverse industry base. Such generalisation and stereotyping would be denounced as prejudice in social settings, and ironically it makes accountability for individuals in such industries who may have been guilty of misconduct that much harder: if everyone is guilty, no one is guilty.

Earlier in this chapter, we highlighted how the 'left' and the 'right' can resemble one another in unhealthy dynamics, specifically short-termist economics. Yet they can also resemble one another in more progressive ways, particularly in charitable and social activity. A visitor from another planet would find it difficult to detect that the community work by a 'conservative' evangelical church in the US was from a different faith background to that of the 'socialist' Sandinista women's groups arranging children's nutrition and education programmes in Nicaragua. You could only see the similarities. In the UK, the Conservative Prime Minister David Cameron has encouraged a renewal of voluntary work and civic duty, arguing that the state cannot meet every need. This has produced a predictable backlash of fury from many political opponents, but received support from the Labour MP Jon Cruddas, traditionally seen as being more 'left' than many of his colleagues.

As a useful guide to the progressive agenda, we would recommend following the example of the trade union Prospect, and using the eight objectives of the United Nations' Millennium Development Goals, which are:

- end poverty and hunger;
- universal education;

- gender equality;
- child health;
- maternal health;
- combat HIV/AIDS;
- environmental sustainability; and
- global partnership.[14]

Can all institutions of the left be certain that they are diligently working towards these goals, to an equal or greater extent than private sector organisations, such as Westpac and Marks & Spencer? The question is not rhetorical or satirical. We think it's a fair test – one that many organisations on the left will pass, but by no means all. The for-profit sector, for example, has much the stronger record in ending poverty, as it generates more jobs, and far more high-quality jobs, that become rewarding, well-remunerated careers. As the Gallup World Poll in 2007[15] found, the desire for a good job is resoundingly the common plea from all peoples as probably the single most important ingredient of improved social and economic well-being for individuals and their families. Recent political upheavals in North Africa and the Middle East probably stem in large part from relatively high unemployment, particularly for young people.

Beliefs around organisational structures and public policy have become solidified into sectarian beliefs. The left assume that a profit-making institution cannot, by definition, concern itself with the wider social good because its sole purpose is to maximise profits. The right assume that good service can never be delivered by a state institution unless it is exposed to competition. Debates rage between proponents of public sector 'reform', which in practice is often a restructure or an introduction of competition, and advocates of state services, many of whom are unwilling to acknowledge waste or poor performance in the services they defend. It is assumed that democracy consists of a robust debate between the two so that the public can judge which is correct. It is possible, however, that both are wrong, because for all the hostility between the two camps, both share the unspoken, and unproven, assumption that type of ownership and institutional structure alone determines the effectiveness of an organisation. Our experience over the years, backed by decades of research studies, shows that the single most important indicator of good service, low waste, social conscience and probity is in the quality of the leadership – a dimension systematically ignored in political discourse, but increasingly on the agenda in corporate circles.

When it comes to leadership of the progressive agenda, left-wing institutions now face competition. That's perfectly healthy, and many left-wing groups pass the test.

---

14   See http://www.un.org/millenniumgoals/graphic.shtml [accessed 28 October 2012].
15   See http://www.gallup.com/strategicconsulting/worldpoll.aspx [accessed 28 October 2012].

But it does pose an interesting challenge for others. As many business-people will confirm, the strongest competition often comes from a totally unexpected direction.

AFTER THE PROTESTS, NOW WHAT?

The Occupy movement in numerous cities has gained huge media coverage in 2011 and 2012, while strikes and protest in Europe have gained in momentum as the debt and euro crises combine in an ugly fashion. It is not always clear what the protestors want, however. An observation made by many journalists talking to Occupy protestors has been that, if you talked to a different protestor, you heard a different agenda. It is easier to say what people are against (inequality, out-of-control banks, cuts to social provision), than what they are for. And because many of the implied remedies mean spending commitments by indebted governments, even the politicians who want to respond have few options.

Being against something isn't enough. There is no guarantee that a different way of running things will be better. Action is dangerous without coherent ideas. The 'Radical Shift' we talk about means a change across the political spectrum, and in their largely failed economic theories. Protest is not a way of life, so the question becomes: now what? We hope that this book contributes to a constructive discussion, and we have sought to include real-life case studies and practical proposals.

THE POLITICAL CLASS – A PROBLEM

While enlightened business leaders are grasping the progressive agenda, the same cannot be said of the political class in the west, and their close friends the editors of broadcast and written media. Party political leaders, whether in government or opposition, remain incurious about the wealth of research and understanding on how to run things better, which is remarkable, when you consider what they do for a living. Ministers, like the executives of the 'business process re-engineering' school, instead prefer to reorganise and rebadge something, rather than improve its operation. Nothing seems to give them more satisfaction than reconfiguring and renaming a ministry, to something sexy containing words like 'innovation' rather than old-fashioned ones like 'industry'. Millions get spent on rebranding and changing the logos, fascias and letterheads. Public sector reform nearly always consists of a restructure, rather than attention to the personnel with responsibility and their skills in leadership and management. Right-wing parties outsource and privatise; left-wing parties nationalise – but from neither side is there anyone saying:

> Hold on a minute, who is running these organisations? Who is handling the private sector contracts? Do we have the necessary IT project managers? Do we have the leadership ability? What is the employee engagement and skills?

The most important matters are deemed junior or 'soft' and are disregarded completely. This needs overturning.

Despite a decade of organisational failures, little attention is paid to their causes. If a bridge collapsed, politicians would call for the best civil engineers to analyse the ruins and identify whether the fault lay in the design, the choice of materials, type of construction, the maintenance schedule or a combination of factors. When the larger part of an entire industry like banking collapses, and imposes colossal cost upon the taxpayer, there is almost nothing by way of a response. There is some heat and noise around bonuses; lame attempts at regulation, but as for understanding the behavioural dynamics and the ideology that encouraged excessive risk and systemic collapse, there is not even a token nod in the right direction. The left is as much to blame as the right, and actually shares many of the beliefs of the flawed ideology that led to crisis, as we have discussed.

We will do everything to prevent a recurrence of economic crisis except, it seems, understand the values, priorities and decision-making processes that created it.

As for the media, one despairs. Richard Donkin, former management columnist at the *Financial Times*, commented at the CMI Management Book of the Year Awards in January 2011, as he collected an award for his book *The Future of Work*, that 'there used to be six of us covering management for national papers – now there are none'. This is like not having political correspondents. In general, coverage of business and management is superficial and inadequate. It is confined to financial reporting – which the media wrongly assume is the same as the business result – and the occasional scandal like BP in the Gulf of Mexico. It is like only covering politics when there is a disaster or a budget, and not bothering with leadership selection, policy commitments, manifesto promises or conferences. The response of the UK paper *The Observer* to the banking crisis was to end the column of its only correspondent, Simon Caulkin, who had warned of the systemic business risk that had been building up in organisational design and management practices!

THE PRODUCTIVE ECONOMY: SHARED NEGLECT

As well as the deeply flawed belief that screwing the workers helps efficiency and profits, another equally damaging shared belief by left and right is the notion that the productive economy is some sort of act of God; that the people who actually make the wealth are just there in the background, taken for granted at best; often hampered by tax and bureaucracy at worst. It is something that politicians make a token nod towards, from time to time. Terms like 'innovation' and 'research and development' sound like things they should be in favour of, but the bulk of their intellectual energy is devoted to spending programmes or pressing monetary levers, as though money just exists, like water falling down a mountainside. In all western governments, the finance minister has vastly more kudos, influence and media profile than the trade minister or the education and skills minister. He or she is almost invariably the deputy president, with the possible exception of the US, where foreign policy might push the Treasury Secretary into third place. In all the talk of European economic divergence, discussion even in the more serious papers obsesses over currency and interest rate policy. Almost nowhere does the thought arise that, perhaps, Germany is more advanced because it has bigger, better run companies, especially in manufacturing. The leaders of France and the EU have for decades insisted that currency alignment, rather than better industrial leadership, is the way to redress this balance.

In the early stages of a developing economy, industrialists and inventors are celebrated. It seems that in post-industrial societies they are relegated to the background. In the US, which has retained a dynamic entrepreneurial sector, especially in mobile and internet technology businesses, the dominant cult of recent years has been 'total shareholder value' – but the understanding of the word 'value' seems to have slipped. Nowadays the definition of the term is skewed towards the interests of those with inherited wealth. 'Value' seems to have become something that a wealthy investor shops around for, rather than something that is created by an inventor or industrialist. The right, just as much as the left, has turned its back on wealth creation.

SHARED BELIEFS

Some shared beliefs of left and right-wing economists and political parties are:

- The economy consists of money; monetary and fiscal policies largely determine the performance of the economy.
- The more you reduce the direct labour cost, the higher the operating margins, company profits and organisational efficiency.
- The size of the state, as measured by the proportion of GDP that it represents, is a major determinant of economic effectiveness and social fairness.
- The ownership structure of a public or private sector organisation is the single biggest determinant in shaping its effectiveness.
- Left and right-wing political opinions are the only possible ones; all other views must be disguised variants thereof.

These beliefs run through everything they say, through every policy they formulate, and every manifesto they lovingly craft and edit. In our years of working with organisations in the public and private sector in different countries of the world, coaching or interviewing employees, managers and business leaders, we have yet to witness any circumstance in which any of the above can be observed and objectively held to be true. In our experience the most significant factors that determine the effectiveness of an organisation or an economy are such matters as leadership calibre, deployment of human capital, incorruptibility of institutions, skills and engagement of the workforce, robustness of contract law, research quality of universities, availability of venture capital and wisdom of investment decisions – factors pretty much excluded from political debate, or relegated to the sidelines as 'nice to have' extras or worthy, common sense areas which sectarian politicians prefer to avoid for fear of having to agree with their opponents.

In addition, each side of the institutional sectarian divide has their own operating myths; but it is remarkable, given the angry rhetoric and mutual dislike, just how large is the overlap of shared belief.

LEFT/RIGHT – RIP

A problem among political leaders and the media is a refusal, certainly in the English-speaking world, to acknowledge that we have beliefs. This unfortunately leaves individuals prey to all manner of unacknowledged ideological beliefs that often emerge in sectarian thought: the beliefs that workers' welfare is the enemy of profit; that ecological protection must mean lower living standards; that performance or ethical conduct depend upon ownership structure, rather than behaviour. These are beliefs that left and right share.

Left and right provide each other with sufficient alibis to inhibit reform. As long as there are enough bad bankers, the left will refuse to acknowledge the damaging effects of excessive borrowing or waste by their institutions. As long as there are restrictive practices, the right will refuse to accept that management, as well as the labour market, requires reform. Both collude in the toxic idea that exploiting the workers maximises profits – something we now know to be fundamentally mistaken; moreover it is a belief that becomes even further departed from reality as the skill levels and interdependence required in advanced businesses increase.

IN SUMMARY

The left/right spectrum is a limited, and often highly distorting, way of understanding real power-plays; and orthodox left and right-wing ideologies share some cynical beliefs that research now shows are false. It is almost worthless. In terms of economic policy, all it tells you is how big or small the state is; nothing on how effective the state may be; how incorruptible; how much it nurtures business development; whether it protects the poor. This 200-year-old reference point, which stems from a short period during the extremely violent French Revolution, is way past its sell-by date. The ideology of the twentieth-century right-wing has failed. But the ideology of the twentieth century left is not the answer – and in some dangerous beliefs, is identical. The left/right duopoly of political thinking misses some of the most important challenges we face. We have to think anew.

FURTHER READING

In this chapter, we have highlighted some examples of how collusion between institutions of the 'left' and the 'right' have contributed to economic instability. By way of balance, in this 'further reading' section we would like to highlight contributions from the respective camps that can have a valuable contribution to make. There is a surprising degree of common ground. *The Competitive Advantage of Nations* and *The Open Veins of Latin America* both illustrate the features of an advanced economy. The two writers highlight the contribution of the state – rather than its size – and the way in which universities, public sector agencies, entrepreneurs and investors combine to create successful business clusters.

Porter, Michael E., *Competitive Advantage of Nations*, Palgrave Macmillan, Second Edition, 1998. First published 1990.

It is a shame that this well-researched tome, rather than the sectarian diatribes of Milton Friedman, has not been the most influential work on business to emerge from conservative quarters. It examines the high degrees of cooperation and skills, and interrelationship between public and private sectors that are required to achieve world-class excellence in a business sector. It showcases diverse examples from the Italian ceramic tile industry to the US patient-monitoring equipment supply side.

Galeano, Eduardo, *Open Veins of Latin America*, Most recent English translation published by Serpent's Tail 2009. First published 1970 by Siglo Veintiuno Editores.

Much of this book concerns the incendiary allegations of imperialist plunder of the resources of Latin America principally by, chronologically, Spain, UK and USA. It had the badge of honour of being banned by the right-wing dictatorships of the 1970s and 1980s. The economic remedy put forward, however, is not state-run socialism, but the opportunity for South America to develop its own successful businesses, supported by a mercantile class, like those in UK and USA.

If you are from a conservative background, and do not wish to touch a book that was given by Hugo Chávez, the Venezuelan President, to President Obama upon the latter's election to office, you may prefer *The Competitive Advantage of Nations*. If you are from a left-wing background, and don't wish your friends see you reading a book by a former adviser to the Reagan Administration, then *Open Veins* may be preferred. There are no longer any jurisdictions, that we are aware of, that ban or inhibit someone from reading both. Of course, in the age of e-readers, it is much more convenient to read a guilty pleasure, as there is no cover!

The fact that two highly intelligent individuals from apparently opposite ends of the left/right spectrum should analyse the dynamics of a successful economy and come to broadly the same conclusions is yet another illustration of the inadequacy of definitions along this spectrum. They both tell the same essential story about business clusters and the development of an advanced economy. What a shame that Chávez does not appear to have read *Open Veins* himself.

CHAPTER 7

CONSCIOUS LEADERSHIP: THE PERSONAL AGENDA

In previous chapters, we have criticised an over-reliance on financial data to understand organisations and economies. We have also discussed the extraordinary persistence of such bias, in spite of the decades of research in organisational theory and management studies that illustrates its weaknesses; which have become more evident given the dominance of financial modelling in the run-up to the banking and economic crisis that emerged in 2007–2008. It is impossible to understand these complex dynamics without discussion of the beliefs that underpin them. Beliefs and culture shape actions and decisions. A different style of leadership that seeks to learn from the recent crisis and prevent recurrence implies attention to all matters: personal conduct as well as parliamentary legislation; business relationships as well as business strategies. We support the concept of 'conscious leadership' based heavily upon Neela Bettridge's work with individual executives and leadership teams, as well as the growing body of research on the matter that both of us have studied.

Traditionally, coaching and personal leadership skills have been considered quite separately from organisational and economic theory. This separation has been arbitrary and unhelpful. It is time to bring them together. It is a particularly common trait in Anglo-Saxon business culture to assume that the dominant beliefs and modus operandi are the only valid ways of perceiving the world and the managerial task, and to be unaware of different perspectives.

Conscious leadership is based on an understanding of the links between different constituencies, or stakeholders, and their mutual interdependence. Traditional MBA-style business education in the late twentieth century chopped the business off from the personal (deemed too soft or self-indulgent) and from societal and environmental considerations (seen as being a matter for politicians and NGOs, not busy executives). This approach has often been criticised as being unethical; it is increasingly evident that it is impractical also. Divorcing business strategy from concern for the planet does not make good business sense over the longer term, because the planet is where the business is located. Disregarding the welfare and ambitions of the workers is a high-risk approach, because ultimately they are responsible for delivering on the promises that the leadership team have made to the customers, the shareholders and other interested parties.

Conscious leadership goes deep into the personal psyche, is extended to colleagues, and reaches out into society. This may sound like a grand or overambitious vision, but it is more realistic. It places the executive in the real context. By illustrating the connections, it can make business leadership more challenging yet also more achievable – one of the many paradoxes of leadership. Conscious leadership has matured as a concept in recent years. We have witnessed a development from seeing social responsibility initially as a compliance or defensive matter, to developing philanthropic activity, to recognising the importance of risk management and being a corporate citizen, to developing a strategic view in which conduct and the brand and reputation are given due consideration as part of social responsibility. The final stage is a systemic view, in which value is created in a shared way. Mark Kramer, one of the proponents of 'shared value', describes this as the difference between a company that purchases fair trade crops to one that works 'in close collaboration with scientists, agronomists, NGOs, governments and even its direct competitors to change the way a crop is grown so that the same farmers can dramatically increase their productivity and income'.[1]

This systemic, holistic approach has also been described, by Bob Willard, as a fundamental shift from the colonialist or twentieth-century business model of 'take–make–waste' to the sustainable practice of 'borrow–use–return'. This means that the conceptual and the practical have to come together, and not be treated in separate ways: beliefs heavily influence conduct, and hence performance. For example, it is a common cultural bias in western management schools, and in business generally, to treat financial figures as 'hard' information, and narrative description as 'soft'. As we discussed in Chapter 1, this bias has contributed to huge misunderstandings on business value and business risk – an apparently positive picture in the quarterly accounts or GDP figures that masked risky or fraudulent practices, with catastrophic results. For managers and business leaders, this has to come back to the personal: do you, as an executive, consider the risk to employee engagement of not making a pay rise, as well as the cost of making one? A pay freeze may still be the necessary option, but the matter has to be considered in this three-dimensional way. Similarly, if an executive is concerned about the cost of coffee from central America, does he or she just look at the prices on the computer screen, or delve into matters such as sustainable farming practices, irrigation, quality of agricultural colleges in the region, deforestation, climate change and so on? Does one read the story or just glance at the headline?

1   See article and online discussion: Elkington, John, Don't abandon CSR for creating shared value just yet, *Guardian Sustainable Business*, 25 May 2011. Available at: http://www. guardian.co.uk/sustainable-business/sustainability-with-john-elkington/corporate-social-resposibility-creating-shared-value [accessed 28 October 2012].

Experience has shown that coaching and 'learning by doing' is the way to develop to a more resilient and sustainable leadership style. If engagement with and understanding of key stakeholders – not just shareholders, but staff, suppliers, the media and so on – it follows that modern commercial leadership has to be understood in a behavioural way, rather than just in terms of analysing business strategy, market position, financial track record and so on – disciplines that are still important, of course.

Between us, we have coached, or interviewed for management books, hundreds of senior executives, and we also have senior management experience ourselves. This is the consistent finding: that personal presence and communication skills do not constitute a sideshow, but lie at the heart of what makes an effective leader.

There is now considerable evidence that the personal presence of a senior business leader has a huge bearing on organisational climate and ultimately business performance. Effective executive development rests on an understanding that the leader brings his or her whole self – or 'way of being' – to the role, and that this can helpfully be defined in three dimensions: language, body and emotion. Moreover, all three have an influence at all times. In Neela Bettridge's experience as an executive coach, this can come as an empowering revelation.

> **Language** – Humans are linguistic beings who are continually speaking and listening. This includes our internal 'chatter', or the conversations that we conduct inside our heads. The content and nature of the conversations we participate in, internally and externally, form an important part of what is real for us. Internal conversations can include familiar 'scripts' that in many cases are hard-wired since childhood. In some cases, these can take the form of limiting beliefs such as: 'I'll never be charismatic', or 'I'm not capable of handling conflict'.
> **Emotion** – Humans are also emotional beings – at all times. Our moods and emotions colour how the world is for us, and predispose us to behave in certain ways. Speaking and listening are integral parts of our behaviour, and thus are influenced by what is going on with us emotionally. Becoming aware of our emotions is hugely empowering.
> **Body** – Our physiology is our physical body, which has an 'inner' and 'outer' dimension. The outer dimension is essentially our posture. How we hold ourselves as persons (for example, self-esteem and self-confidence) is reflected in how we hold our bodies. Our inner body is the working of our internal systems (for example, respiratory system) and our organs.

There is a reluctance to acknowledge even that we have beliefs, much less that they influence actions. This is especially true in the still largely mono-lingual Anglo-Saxon world, where it is commonly taken for granted that all the big issues of how the world operates, what business or the market constitutes and how they can best be understood and analysed, have been settled. The seismic events of autumn 2008 ought to have shattered that complacency, but there are worrying signs of business as usual – at least in the political space, as we discuss in Chapter 8. Faith in improved performance through competition and measured by the quarterly financial report; in the tendency towards equilibrium of deregulated finance; in flexible labour markets to be able to absorb all necessary adjustments in performance; in the un-improvability of business management in a free economy; in the rationale of treating employees as disposable resources, and commodities as infinite in supply, have all been exposed as flawed and dangerous in the past few years. Yet faith in these ill-founded notions has not been extinguished. Partly, it persists because some of the political alternatives being put forward are even worse, as we shall discuss in Chapter 8. But this is not a sufficient excuse. At an individual level, an increasing number of business leaders are reassessing their beliefs, and updating them to bring them in line with a complex reality of faulty market pricing, finite commodities and the nature of the company as a complex community of skilled human beings.

Within business, there are some signs of progress, and growing awareness of a holistic approach, or 'conscious leadership'. There is now a significant body of knowledge, applied learning and research behind this approach. Two examples from Neela's coaching work illustrate the type of development that can come about with this model.

CASE STUDY 1

Transition to a Senior Role within a Multinational Firm

In this coaching intervention, the individual is a former sales director, who had been an extremely successful sales director, and who then took on a senior international executive role. It required him to work cross-culturally, and to step up to a role at international board level – two major challenges.

Neela watched him in-situ; at board meetings, and arranged a series of more formal assessments. What emerged was that he could come across as somewhat aloof. In meetings he would close down the discussion; while he would say that he welcomed contributions, the moment someone said something he would close it down, and his body language emphasised that he didn't want someone to comment.

This mattered not just for him but for the organisation: it was going through a major shift from being a national firm to being a global organisation. He could not stay where he was, and nor could the company. Neela challenged him on his behaviour – in a safe and where possible humorous way. She also used role-play: in a coaching session, pretending to be different people that he was meeting. He also watched himself on video – an extremely powerful method.

What emerged was that he had a fear that if he shared too much information everyone would climb aboard the bandwagon and the management of the company would become uncontrollable. Another crucial discovery was that he assumed that all conflict was aggressive. Neela pointed out that conflict can be constructive, and encouraged him to have managed, facilitated discussions with senior colleagues who disagreed with one another about the future direction of the organisation. This process led both to better decisions and to more understanding of the direction taken.

She encouraged him to have a lot of one-to-one conversations and to walk the floor; getting out among the organisation, and talking. Neela also worked with the client on developing the direction and vision for the organisation, and encouraging the other business leaders to share in that.

He ended up being a very effective CEO and, for all Neela's challenging questions, they ended up with a strong relationship based on mutual respect.

CASE STUDY 2

A High-performing Senior Team in the Oil Industry

A large multinational company in the oil industry hired Neela to develop their senior team. She was set a challenging task to take their team from being a very well-performing team to being a super-performing team. The company wanted her to help them build a better understanding of how to enhance the brand and build on existing skills, values, purpose amd mission. It was about looking at this team and tweaking it: what is each member of this team contributing?

She explored in depth the values and context of stakeholders in four dimensions: the individual's personality and strengths; the individual's way of being in the world; the organisation's characteristics and strengths; and the external context in which it was operating. She also did some futures work, and scenario planning, discussing not only mismatches between current strengths and business requirements, but how these were likely to alter along certain possible changes in the context.

What was developed was a way of operating that would serve them better in terms of a high-performing team. The work included very intensive teamwork, including outward-bound activities, and creative work; building the collective problem-solving capabilities. In this way they strengthened their systemic thinking and collective self-awareness; coming to an understanding of the potential and the limitations of the team.

> *Neela gave us a better understanding of where we can enhance personal brand and fully build on existing skills. We also identified key traits and behaviours that can at times limit our performance but also areas where we can build on key strengths.*

For the most part, this learning – about language, emotion, body – is applied in a pragmatic way to assist individual executives become more effective; it is more than just personal development for its own sake. An authoritative presence so that people in the organisation automatically look to the leader for reassurance and guidance has much more impact than has been recognised historically. Even attention to seemingly minor items, such as the ability to listen and prioritise, for example, or intonation and choice of phrase when delivering an important address to the workforce, or the media or to shareholders, can be decisive.

Yet the effectiveness of such a holistic approach to an executive role begs profound questions about our wider understanding of business and organisational leadership. If beliefs, conduct and even bodily posture and tone of voice affect organisational performance, then we are firmly in the realm of a behavioural understanding of organisational dynamics. This is profoundly different from the mechanistic description of the firm that have been standard on the MBA curriculum, where market position, strategic analysis, financial management and marketing have dominated, and the content described above dismissed as 'soft' and the subject of optional modules – though to be fair many MBA providers have been amending their programmes in recent years to rebalance the curriculum.

What also emerges is that a rounded approach in which the leader understands the interests of different stakeholders, and seeks their engagement, is profoundly different from the cynical beliefs of agency theory, or the economic orthodoxies that minimising workers' pay and conditions maximises profit margins. These beliefs still have considerable influence upon major decisions. It is still quite common for corporations to make a decision on outsourcing, for example, including of sensitive operations such as customer contact centres, largely on the basis of the operational costs. In the real world, however, a company's customers stay with it on the basis primarily of the service they receive, delivered by the staff.

This is a Copernican shift in miniature: the twentieth-century MBA model assumed that finance and measurable transactional costs are 'real' or 'hard' and that employee engagement and customer relationships were 'soft' or even 'intangible', yet the latter can produce costs of a far greater dimension. People – staff and customers – exist; it is the financial report that is intangible. Hence we now witness 'onshoring', as companies realise that, for example, difficulties in understanding certain accents, or time differences, generate costs far greater than those that were saved because the hourly wage rate was x per cent lower.

We cannot escape belief. Policies, strategies, political ideas and cost analysis are all heavily influenced by our beliefs, which determine the types of analysis we use and, above all, the matters we choose to prioritise over others. Beliefs determine the 'frame', or terms of reference, we use to make sense of the world.

SCRIPTS: THE STORIES WE TELL OURSELVES

We often carry with us deeply held *a priori* notions of the relative importance of financial versus narrative information. What matters more than having the 'correct' or most balanced approach as an individual is to be conscious of one's biases; conscious that they are individual and that no one is omniscient, and ideally to have diversity of background in management teams, and to be able to chair and facilitate debate and discussion on the matters. This does not then, to stress, mean leaping to the other extreme, pretending that emotions are all we need to worry about and financial discipline can be relaxed. Rather, it is about moving from a two-dimensional understanding of business costs and risks to a three-dimensional one. An understanding in three dimensions involves an understanding of the strengths, weaknesses and emotions of managers, leaders and other employees.

Belief determines our assumptions around the efficiency of the private sector, or the munificence of the public; of the primacy of financial data or the way to handle difficult employees. It determines the importance we attach to relationships with our colleagues, the pay and morale of employees throughout the organisation, and the importance of communication.

So the common but misleading beliefs that have led management theory to go astray, that we discussed in Chapter 3, have been imprinted upon the circuit boards of many aspiring business leaders – physics envy and the worship of data; agency theory; the belief that a social conscience is optional baggage for a corporation to carry; the underplaying of the importance of interdependence. In the example of Case Study 1, the belief of the executive that only the tiny senior cadre should have access to important information indicates some of these beliefs may have been influential: the downplaying of interdependence, for example, and the notion of the company as a machine that obeys certain laws of physics, piloted by a small team with exclusive access to the most important information.

We bring with us operating assumptions, *a priori* beliefs, to every role, and this includes the senior executive, the trade union negotiator, the green campaigner. The way in which management is taught seems to assume a hermetic seal between the world of work and the rest of life. This is consistent with the 'machine' metaphor. If all we are doing is operating a few levers to manoeuvre the corporate vehicle, it is logical to ignore our emotion, background, philosophy, internalised scripts, attitude and behaviour. But these will still be having an impact. A senior manager who rarely leaves his or her office, devoting hours to studying the finances, and never communicates directly with the workforce, is still having an emotional impact – actually a huge impact – upon the workforce. It is just going to be a negative one, which will very probably convert itself into negative outcomes in terms of team and company performance. Then the financial figures deteriorate and the phrase 'vicious circle' comes to mind.

Working experience and formal management training are not the only influences on our way of being as a manager or other professional. It is likely that extra-curricular influences have had at least as much impact. Consider this: who had more influence upon your attitude towards work, careers and ambition, and your views on the role of corporations or of central government; your parents or your MBA tutor? These values are carried with us into the workplace, into senior roles, in the private conversations we have with ourselves, and betraying themselves in our conversations, ability to engage in conversations; even our bodily posture.

It is well chronicled, for example, that a very high proportion of male presidents and prime ministers lost their fathers at a young age. This straightforward, biographical observation illustrates how leadership abilities and attainment have explanations that are deeply psychodynamic in nature, to do with internalised scripts and our 'way of being', in addition to matters such as academic qualifications and formal attainments. This recognition is well understood by biographers and obituary writers, but not fully into the development of managers.

This is why coaching is increasingly being used in executive circles: it is not some form of 'therapy-for-suits', rather it is based on the recognition that in practice the whole personality is at play in the leadership role. To a significant extent, it reflects the lack of preparation for a senior role that many executives experience. While some corporations are addressing this with development programmes and formal succession planning, progress is patchy. Many senior managers may have spent years qualifying in accountancy, engineering or marketing, but have only spent a few 'away-days' on how to handle people and step up to a senior role.

The influence of the MBA principle that management is little more than an analytical technique and that if you can manage one type of organisation you can manage any, is now exposed as deeply flawed.

Some common internalised scripts are:

- Management is a rational process. There is no place for emotion.
- I must control everything in order to be effective.
- An idea or project must be perfect before it can be shared.
- The shareholders are the only or most important audience.
- Financial information is more reliable than narrative description.

These scripts reflect the dominant culture. If the culture were to change, others might rise to the surface, including potentially damaging ones. A health warning to issue here is that business leadership should not become unbalanced in the opposite direction: financial responsibility and rational decision making remain of fundamental importance. The degree of managerial control over staff should be optimised, not minimised. Employee engagement is generally positive, but can spill over into irrational exuberance. Every strength is also a weakness. The purpose of conscious leadership is to place both traditional and less familiar managerial disciplines in a broader, more realistic context, not prioritise some excessively over others. Nor is it helpful to segregate rational analysis from other dimensions of leadership.

A common phenomenon in recent years has been an approach to leadership that segregates ethical or sustainable matters from what are perceived to be 'hard' business concerns such as market position, acquisitions strategy and financial analysis. The segregation is arbitrary and unhelpful. In the real world, everything is linked. Ultimately, financial results and market share are a consequence of the human interactions between staff and customers, while mergers and acquisitions depend upon a good cultural fit and engagement, and the development of a shared vision and effective teamwork.

Curiously, however, while the behavioural, emotional and psychological dimensions of leadership have been downplayed in the MBA curriculum and in the business news pages, it is something that many senior executives, entrepreneurs and investors take very seriously indeed. Many of the most successful have always done so, but have relied more on experience and 'nous' than formal psychological profiling. While the financial orientation is still almost ubiquitous in many corporations, private equity investors are more eclectic. David Cooper's book *Leadership Risk: A Guide for Private Equity and Strategic Investors*[2] makes what ought to be the fairly obvious point that the single biggest element of risk in an investment is typically the performance of the leadership team, which in turn is influenced considerably by their personalities and the relationships between them. It is impossible to make a comprehensive assessment without some analysis of motivation, leadership style, personal ambition, communication abilities and so on. For example, is the venture central to the proposed CEO's ambitious career plan, or is he or she wealthy and semi-retired, regarding it almost as a hobby? Is the individual comfortable and experienced working in a team, or a perfectionist solo operator with a short temper? The success of the enterprise can depend as much on these considerations as on the quality of the product or the business processes. Indeed, often there is little to differentiate between companies on the latter considerations, and more to gain or lose by studying and understanding leadership qualities and teamwork abilities in the company; ideally not just in the top cadre but throughout the organisation.

One reason why the evidence base showing the benefits of an engaged workforce have not had more influence is that it is in competition with a rival theory; that it is the disengaged workforce that is most profitable. As discussed elsewhere in this book, such an idea has its roots in economic and political theory, but has not been founded on a base of evidence.

---

2   Cooper, David, *Leadership Risk: A Guide for Private Equity and Strategic Investors*, John Wiley, 2010.

Enlightened ideas around sustainability or employee engagement have often been grafted on to more established management models based on a machine-like metaphor for the business consisting of resources, cost and outputs, as though the two were compatible. Internalised scripts around the primacy of data, the unimportance of employee morale, the preference for command and control, go unchallenged and remain dominant in the collective executive mental circuitry. The engagement theory of profits has struggled to be established, because it has been in competition with the disengagement theory. As discussed in Chapter 3 (subheading 'Misreading of Politics, and Business Process Re-engineering'), the theory that efficient business practices result from treating workers as no more than a cost or a disposable resource became fashionable in the 1990s and early 2000s, despite research evidence supporting a more enlightened leadership approach. In some firms, the two competing ideologies coexist uncomfortably. It is common to come across companies where managers practise the doctrine of low pay, surveillance and minimum trust for much of the time, but then expect teams to be enthused by an away-day or an employee awards event. The result is confusion.

Indeed, it may even be better to have a 'traditional' approach to management, and do so consistently, than to give a pretence of conversion to a more people-based philosophy, but to do so inconsistently or insincerely. In a similar way, veterans from the management and the union side of partnership deals, where the principle is that the union seeks to help the business win orders and jobs and may even have a place on the board, stress that this approach depends upon a high level of trust. Without this, it is probably better to have traditional negotiations and bargaining.

This is why we encourage a whole-hearted approach to leadership, encompassing language, emotion and body; recognising the importance of beliefs and their impact on conduct, and developing an understanding of the role of all stakeholders. Groucho Marx is reported to have quipped that: 'Sincerity is the key – if you can fake that, you've got it made'. But faking won't work for long in business.

GENDER, RISK AND LEADERSHIP

Discussion of behavioural dynamics in business would not be complete without some reference to gender. The extreme risks taken in many trades in financial markets, including in products that traders did not understand but were too proud to admit, is arguably more of a male trait. One could widen this more generally to the cult of short-termism and management by quarterly return that has been dominant in the past two decades.

In the case of the markets, it is now well established that traders experience extreme emotions of fear, greed and irrational exuberance, with monetary gains triggering the same cognitive responses as the short-lived euphoria from a drug like cocaine or morphine.[3] Understanding these phenomena could lead to better understanding of asset price booms and busts, which have had seriously destabilising effects on human societies for centuries, being major causatory factors of historical events, including even the Great Depression and the Second World War, which followed the Roaring Twenties culminating in the Wall Street Crash, as well as the crisis we are currently living through. Probably the most comprehensive overview of the history is the superbly titled *This Time is Different*, by Carmen Reinhart and Kenneth Rogoff.[4]

Arguably men, fuelled by the aggressive competitive ingredient testosterone, take more risks than women. So would a more female trading floor and risk department help smooth these destructive booms and busts? There are health warnings to issue with such a line of thought, given the dangers of stereotyping and the huge variation within gender, but it is an intriguing idea. The UK feminist politician Harriet Harman received ridicule in 2011 for suggesting that Lehman Brothers might have survived if it had been 'Lehman Sisters', but she was able to point out that the very same idea was taken more seriously when put forward by two male Conservatives a short while later. Nadhim Zahawi and Matthew Hancock, authors of *Masters of Nothing: How the Crash Will Happen Again Unless We Understand Human Nature*, stated: 'The current gender imbalance seems to be contributing to the kind of market manias which cause financial crises. The dominance by men does not exist because of the inherently masculine nature of finance. Rather, the masculine nature of finance exists because of its dominance by men'.[5]

Sadly, this foray into a behavioural understanding of economics, and a shared understanding across party political lines, appears not to be the dominant theme as the political tribes revert to their simplistic debates of 'growth versus austerity' or regulation versus deregulation or big state versus small state (see Chapter 8).

The bigger point is the behavioural one, rather than gender, but it is highly likely that a more balanced, diverse boardroom will generate more eclectic viewpoints, richer discussions and a fuller view of markets and of business risk. There is an emerging agenda common to regulation of the banks and the financial markets; promotion of women to senior corporate positions, and promotion of the interests of employees throughout organisations. In all three areas, legislation has often been the chosen route of campaigners seeking respectively better risk management in the markets, more diverse corporate leadership, and fairness and good careers for staff.

---

3   Lo, Andrew W., Fear, Greed and Financial Crises: A Cognitive Neurosciences Perspective, MITSloan Management, October 2011. Available at: https://mitsloan.mit.edu/finance/pdf/Lo-20120109d.pdf [accessed 28 October 2012].

4   Reinhart, Carmen and Rogoff, Kenneth, *This Time is Different: Eight Centuries of Financial Folly*, Princeton University Press, 2009.

5   Testosterone to blame for banking crash, say Tory MPs, *The Independent*, 4 September 2011. Available at: http://www.independent.co.uk/news/uk/politics/testosterone-to-blame-for-banking-crash-say-tory-mps-2348912.html [accessed 28 October 2012].

While legislation can be effective at curbing the worst behaviour, it is much less effective – some would argue, counter-productive – at encouraging the best. All three areas are characterised by social dynamics too complex for fine-tuning by law. Attempts to do so can end up being intricate or heavy-handed, resulting in Byzantine complexity, unintended consequences, token representation, stultifying fear of prosecution, or a combination of all. The issue of employee rights will be discussed further in Chapter 8 on New Populism, as it is so close to the development of political and economic ideas from political parties and in business education.

It is our conclusion that a gender balance at senior levels of business is a highly worthwhile objective, and has been shown to be beneficial for organisations and for society in pioneering countries such as Norway. There may be a role for guidance and regulation, but the overwhelming challenge is cultural and behavioural. This is also an area where Neela Bettridge has considerable experience as a female executive and entrepreneur, and as an executive coach who has coached women in senior roles. While no style of behaviour is uniform across each gender, she has noted a stronger distaste in female professionals for engaging in office politics. This is likely to be one of several factors that have inhibited promotion to senior levels, including board level. She has coached women to learn that the appropriate use of influence, such as building a constituency of support, is perfectly legitimate within organisational life. Indeed, many colleagues welcome and respect this in potential leaders, provided it is done in an authentic and honest way. This behavioural dimension also implies changes for organisations and for male leaders.

The other obvious dimension of diversity relates to different cultures. The MBA is an Anglo-Saxon product, and our experience is that many managers in the English-speaking world are insufficiently aware of different world-views, assuming their 'taken-for-granted' assumptions are universal. There are some straightforward remedies for this: working abroad and learning another language are the best. If this is impractical, then daily disciplines such as reading the news and about business in different sources – for example, China or India-based media, many of which are in English. Philip Whiteley has researched and co-authored two books on this, with international executive coach Susan Bloch.[6]

CUSTOMER ENGAGEMENT

One commercial argument for greater diversity is the desire to reflect the customer base. There must be very few companies that have a mostly white, male customer base – golf club manufacturers perhaps, and even here the picture is changing markedly – so it is unlikely that a leadership cadre skewed towards one slice of the

---

6   Bloch, Susan and Whiteley, Philip, *How to Manage in a Flat World*, Pearson, 2007; and Bloch, Susan and Whiteley, Philip, *The Global You*, Marshall Cavendish, 2011.

demographic is going to be optimal for business performance. In consumer goods, for example, women make up by far the majority of decision makers; increasingly in financial services also. So it makes obvious sense to have women in leading roles in the organisation; in board-level and functional head roles, and not only in junior sales and advertising positions. The rise of the middle class in emerging economies, and the relative decline of the indebted western economies, means that some of the most lucrative consumer markets are increasingly in Asia, South America, eastern Europe, the Middle East and Africa.

One of the most revealing ways of approaching the whole diversity issue is to do some scenario sketching and invert the onus: suppose that in 30 years' time the boards of major companies are diverse in gender and cultural background, serving an international and socially diverse customer base, how would you pitch a proposal to revert to a white, male, profile? It would appear ridiculous. So the question 'why should we *not* be diverse?' can be more telling than the question 'why diversity?'

This links to the wider point about customer relationships, and the direct links to diversity of make-up, leadership conduct, clarity of communication and purpose within the organisation and employee engagement. There is a fairly logical virtuous circle that long-term, highly respected firms like Whole Foods and WL Gore exhibit. The more your employees are engaged, actually wanting the customer to be well served and the company to succeed, and the higher their skill-levels necessary to do this, the stronger your demand. This leads to higher levels of repeat business – much more cost-effective than other types of business owing to reduced marketing spend, a better reputation for the brand, more satisfied and well-rewarded employees whose engagement levels rise further.

Most people understand this – but in some cases, only in certain contexts. There is insufficient wider awareness that the logic of this value chain, based on ethical conduct and company reputation, is not always consistent with finance-based analysis and some of the fads and trends critiqued in Chapter 3. And, as discussed earlier in this chapter, the engagement theory of profits has been at war with the disengagement model, which has been the dominant theory in recent decades.

THE PARADOX OF LEADERSHIP

Partial or uneven commitments to conscious leadership are derived in large part in the segregation of leadership studies from organisational studies, and the dominance of mechanistic metaphors and the language of finance to the latter. Hence in this book we encourage an approach in which all aspects of organisational life, including all stakeholders, are seen together, and as being directly linked to leadership. This can assist the virtuous circle of the best companies, as discussed above, and can also help guard against irrational exuberance, or hubris.

One of the problems with the mechanistic modelling and dominance of finance is that such an approach excludes consideration of paradox, complexity and the unintended consequence. In the MBA on this simplistic model, it is assumed that if you set a strategy and go for it, you achieve it. A study just over a decade ago by KPMG indicated that a staggering 80 per cent of company mergers had not achieved their objectives, yet the very same proportion of executives involved *believed that that had done so.*[7] With this level of self-deception clearly quite common in corporate leadership circles, perhaps the credit crisis was only a matter of time.

At the heart of 'conscious leadership' is the concept of knowing oneself and one's context. The wise leader knows the limit of his or her powers. He or she has read Shakespeare and Cervantes as well as the *Harvard Business Review*, and understands that the paradox of leadership is the same as the paradox of existence: that we have less control than we want, but more than we can handle. This is the meta theme for all drama, and can be equally well described in the language of Freud as in literature. The unintended consequences of our decisions can be greater than intended, and often through no fault of our own. The former British Prime Minister Harold Macmillan was being honest, not helpless when he described the biggest challenge of being at the head of government as, 'Events, dear boy, events'.

The effective leader is humble as well as authoritative. This is a paradox. The effective leader is good at handling paradox. John Mackey, co-founder of Whole Foods, talks of the 'paradox of profit' (see Chapter 8), that it is not maximised by making maximisation your goal; rather by seeing profit as a happy by-product of producing socially valuable goods and services and doing so in a sustainable and ethical manner.

There is a fear that if you engage your emotions, deploy your empathy, communicate well with your staff and care about engagement, that you will become unable to steel yourself for the difficult decisions. In any organisations, redundancies will be necessary sometimes, pay freezes will have to be imposed, benefits cut back. The best companies, like Southwest Airlines, WL Gore, Whole Foods and so on, will do so as a last resort; will have sound business reasons for the decisions and communicate them well. They understand that the way in which they handle such decisions sends out messages to any departing staff, their friends, their customers. They also understand that they may wish to re-hire those folk one day, and maintain the morale of those who stay. And because such firms are well run, over the longer term they have to make fewer such tough calls than others.

---

7   Unlocking Shareholder Value, KPMG 1999. Available at: http://www.imaa-institute. org/docs/m&a/kpmg_01_Unlocking%20Shareholder%20Value%20-%20The%20Keys%20 to%20Success.pdf [accessed 25 June 2012].

However, an unfortunate binary delusion emerges in presentation of leadership styles, in which 'tough', macho style is contrasted with the empathic emotionally intelligent style. Much journalistic reporting of business leadership features the contrast of a ruthless boss and the nice boss, wrapping each leader up in a monochrome cloak. This is a false choice. There is nothing soft about engaging with the emotions of yourself or of your team, and it doesn't mean ducking the tough decisions. Being an effective leader means being both empathic and tough, as part of understanding the paradox of leadership. Making the decision on which is appropriate depends upon the context and judgement, rather than the leader's mood, which is why understanding of emotions is so important.

Much as we love the brilliant writing of Lucy Kellaway in the *Financial Times*, we must take issue with the presentation of this choice between tough and soft in her column a few years ago, in which she claimed that a fashion of avoiding fear in the workplace had gotten out of hand:

> *For the last two decades there has been only one view on management and leadership, and that is the squidgy-soft view. This reached a peak 10 years ago with Daniel Goleman's book Emotional Intelligence, which argues that what leaders need in the workplace is empathy, and since then no one has dared challenge it.*[8]

This is to misquote Goleman. His model does allow for a coercive style – but in certain contexts and for short periods, such as when a workforce has become complacent and competitive pressures have suddenly increased. A coercive style sustained for any length of time is corrosive to morale and tends to be accompanied by declining service standards. There is some tacit recognition of this in a tendency to recognise some interim leaders as being effective for a turnaround situation, but a less appropriate hire for a long-term post.

IN SUMMARY

Conscious leadership means understanding that one's unconscious beliefs affect prioritising, strategy-setting and decisions in business, and also personal leadership style such as presentational or negotiating skills. It means opening a dialogue with one's internalised 'scripts', and recognising the strengths and weaknesses of their contribution, while encouraging enquiry into other ways of seeing the world.

---

8   Kellaway, Lucy, Managers need the S-Factor, *Financial Times*, 12 March 2006. Available at: http://www.ft.com/cms/s/1/a52c7b0c-b1dc-11da-96ad-0000779e2340.html# axzz1x8zSjrdT [accessed 28 October 2012].

Leadership development needs to encompass all dimensions: personal, relational, analytical and political. The approach of recent decades to segregate personal, ethical, commercial, social and environmental matters has failed and needs to change, not only for ethical purposes, but in order to reflect the reality of an interdependent world. Leaders can and do improve their performance; this is best done as part of a continuous, integrated approach to all leadership dimensions.

Becoming conscious is not a cure-all, but it is an improvement on being unconscious.

CHAPTER 8

NEW POPULISM AND THE DANGERS

The failure of market deregulation and neo-liberal business models has led to the dangerous idea that any alternative must be better. Recent political developments include the rise of nationalist–populist movements which, in our view, do not provide the antidote and in some cases increase unfairness, mismanagement and inequality – especially inequality between generations. The route to fairness lies in developing participative, ethically-run organisations in the public and private sector, not in protectionism or unsustainable borrow-and-spend policies.

In Chapter 1, we discussed the cognitive bias of the 'binary delusion' – the mistaken belief that, if a policy has failed, something stridently different must automatically be better, and that we should continue applying that approach even if it also fails. There is an analogy with medical history. In the First World War, a young Scottish doctor began to be frustrated by the exclusive use of antiseptics to treat infected wounds. They were worse than useless, he concluded; actually having the effect of weakening the injured soldier's immune system, many of whom died of sepsis as a result. Alexander Fleming wrote a paper on the subject for *The Lancet*, and decided that a completely different approach was needed. After the war he dedicated himself to researching anti-bacterial agents and, a decade later, made his discovery of penicillin.

We know that deregulated financial markets and the neo-liberal ideology have failed, but the antidote is not state socialism or other variants of nationalist–populist politics: they just weaken the patient further. We need to discover our antibiotics.

It is our conclusion that the 'penicillin' for business and politics is the recognition that the interests of workers and the environment are not in opposition to the interests of business owners and managers. From this apparently small recognition big things flow, and everything has to change.

Unfortunately, in the mean time nationalist–populist parties have been on the rise, especially in Europe. Much of their rhetoric involves denouncing international capitalists, particularly 'Anglo-Saxon speculators'. Given the record of some investment banks, with the excessive credit creation and fraudulent Ponzi schemes such as the trade in Collatorised Debt Obligations (CDO), it is understandable that such references strike a chord, especially as ordinary taxpayers are left to pick up the bill. But the nationalist–populists do not offer a radical break, and in some ways their policies would mean an even more extreme version of the same policy options that have failed over the past few years. Consider the manifestos of Marine Le Pen of the National Front and Jean-Luc Mélenchon of the Left Front, who between them gathered nearly 30 per cent of the popular vote in the first round of the French Presidential election in April 2012. They offer further confirmation of the near-uselessness of the 'left/right' spectrum as a way of understanding politics: though they would regard themselves as being opposite ends of this spectrum and clearly dislike each other, their platforms resemble one another more than they differ. Both called for retirement at 60, for rises in the minimum wage, upped the anti-EU polemic, and denounced international capitalists and the 'system'. They pepper their speeches with references to historical French working-class heroes, especially Joan of Arc and the Jacobins. Le Pen called for exit from the euro, but arguably Mélenchon was even more nationalistic – as much of the cost of his entitlement spending would effectively be passed to German, Dutch and Finnish taxpayers through the shared currency.

Mélenchon called for 100 per cent tax rates above €360,000. In the end, the presidential winner François Hollande intends, at the time of writing, to go some way towards that with a top tax rate of 75 per cent. This has prompted a rush for the exit by wealthy French people to Switzerland, Belgium and London, where the Battersea and Chelsea district is now referred to as the twenty-first arrondisement. Hollande is also planning reductions in retirement age in the public sector, an uncosted policy of economic entitlement for a country with high and rising life expectancy, a budget deficit and a national debt approaching 100 per cent of GDP. The cost of this policy would most likely have to be funded with the help of government borrowing; it cannot simply be assumed that the costs of economic entitlements are always minor, or always fall upon the rich, as we shall discuss later in this chapter. A possible effect of Hollande's policies, launched amid much denunciation of Anglo-Saxon speculators, could be a wholesale transfer of wealth from French taxpayers to investment banks based in London – a significant and growing proportion of whose employees are wealthy French tax exiles. This is not to say the policy is necessarily unaffordable and will automatically end this way; rather to encourage a look through the wide-angle lens in which all transfers of wealth are assessed.

Policies such as a high statutory minimum wage, early retirement and other Mélenchon ideas, such as making it unlawful for profitable companies to make redundancies, often sound radical, but are insubstantial if they become unaffordable. It is relatively easy for politicians to pass a law specifying a certain wage or job guarantee, often without sufficient attention to whether or not employment prospects actually improve for working people. What really makes a difference is the less glamourous, patient work in building participative businesses that offer sustainable employment and rewarding careers – an endeavour that can only be effectively done by public and private sectors working together.

In Spain, one witnesses the left-wing trade unions march against the *reforma laboral*, in support of Franco-era bureaucratic systems that almost certainly contribute to maintaining high levels of unemployment – for decades much higher in Spain than in comparable economies in Europe. It is true, as we have written elsewhere, that management reform is often more important than 'labour market reform', but there does come a point at which workplace regulation can have a detrimental impact on job creation, and should be optimised, not maximised – from the workers' point of view, as much as the managers. The interests are closer than conventional political and economic theories permit.

The Le Pen/Mélenchon approach accepts as a given the notion that it is always in the business interest to pay low wages, and that only the state can offer protection. We now know this belief to be mistaken, which is why, as writers with primarily a business and management background, we march boldly and unapologetically into the political arena: we have discovered something of huge potential benefit for political and economic policy-making and for voters. We have found our penicillin. Pursuing the comparison with medicine, it is remarkable how keen we human beings are to build upon evidence and discovery in the sciences, but show no similar interest in business and politics, where practices are still based upon folklore, Medieval accounting systems and nationalistic sentiment.

Politically, by offering such appalling alternatives to the neo-liberal model, politicians such as Le Pen and Mélenchon help to let investment banks off the hook for their recent financial crimes. There is a danger, even a likelihood, that the calls for 'growth not austerity' will mean a return to short-termism and debt as a response to a crisis brought about by short-termism and debt. The entire 'growth versus austerity' debate rests on the beliefs that wealth is not created by business, that economics is not caused by behaviour and that organisations are not run by people. Moderate politicians believe this and the nationalist–populists even more so.

No western nation has held a full, open and thorough public debate about the causes of the crisis. In the UK, for example, thousands of hours of Parliamentary and judicial inquiry time have been devoted to unearthing the extent to which a few tabloid journalists broke the law by hacking into the phones of celebrities and a few other unfortunate individuals caught up in news events. This may be a necessary endeavour, but there has been no commensurate inquiry into the root causes – cultural, political, economic – of the recent banking and economic crisis, the effects of which will last for at least a generation and which is affecting everyone. It is back to 'business as usual', with the grotesque nationalist–populist figures providing cover for the banks to escape their duty to reform.

At the point of writing, however, some moves in the direction of public inquiry have belatedly begun. Following the eruption of the scandal of alleged rigging of the London Inter-Bank Offered Rate (LIBOR) by Barclays and other banks, which emerged in June 2012, fines have been levied in the USA, criminal prosecutions may follow, and the British Government established a Parliamentary inquiry – the opposition Labour Party called for a judicial inquiry. There were two related scandals: one concerned apparent under-reporting of LIBOR to retain confidence in the bank at the height of the credit crisis in 2008. The other, much more serious, charge was that individual traders deliberately rigged the rate in order to help their own traders.

What was a revelation to many of us who do not work in the City was that an indicator as influential as LIBOR should rely on Mediaeval practices such as self-declaration, rather than be based on hard transactional data. This reflects the casual self-regulatory ideology that has guided the approach to financial services and business management in the past couple of decades.

The responses are welcome, but the wider need is for a renewed political culture that sees economics as behavioural, and treats financial services like any other. This means holding a much broader enquiry into the ideologies, beliefs and political practices that have supported extreme short-termism and irrational exuberance, as well as the workings of particular parts of the banking industry.

There is a tendency to regard financial services as a separate world, where separate rules apply: it is either worshipped or demonised, according to prejudices of the right or the left. The better approach is to treat it like any other business; to demystify it. It was common at times during the Barclays controversy for commentators to bemoan the lack of regulatory power to hold LIBOR-fixers to account. This is nonsense. No western nation has exempted any industries or individuals from prosecution for fraud. If there is evidence of fraud, that must be the charge, something which the UK's Serious Fraud Office has begun to explore, at the point of writing.

When economics and organisational management are viewed behaviourally, based on an understanding of the ideologies that guide decisions, the LIBOR scandal becomes less surprising. Almost certainly, more banking scandals will emerge over the coming years, as the losers from CDO trading, LIBOR fixing and other excesses from the age of irrational exuberance seek recompense. These practices flow from the business model of the past two decades, and follow the accountancy scandals, and mega-merger fiascos, as described in Chapter 1.

A blunt overview of Europe's crisis has been given by Raghuram Rajam, a former IMF chief economist: 'For decades before the financial crisis in 2008, advanced economies were losing their ability to grow by making useful things. But they needed to somehow replace the jobs that had been lost to technology and foreign competition and to pay for the pensions and health care of their ageing populations. So in an effort to pump up growth, governments spent more than they could afford and promoted easy credit to get households to do the same'.[1]

Few of his fellow economists, and even fewer newspaper columnists or politicians, are prepared to describe the dilemma in such a frank manner. Europe is giving up on austerity, and opting for denial. It's not going to be pretty. The economic debate is portrayed as a choice of 'growth versus austerity', in which 'growth' is a euphemism for more government borrowing. This is a false choice, based on a refusal to learn the lessons of the recent past. Many commentators say that austerity is 'not working'. Well of course it isn't! It's like saying that falling over doesn't 'work' as a cure for drunkenness. The only real cure is not to get drunk again. Austerity isn't supposed to 'work'. It is not a medicine; rather, it is an inevitable by-product of reckless credit creation, dysfunctional banks, unchecked speculative markets, a failed neo-liberal business model and wasteful governments. Returning to such practices will only mean more and even greater 'austerity' a short way down the road.

Reform of the banks has been limited and piecemeal – much less thorough and effective than the Glass-Steagall reforms of the Roosevelt administration following the credit bubble and depression of the 1920s and 1930s, but which were reversed in the 1990s, with disastrous consequences a decade later.

The behavioural causes of crisis are simply ignored, and it seems to be in the mutual short-term interest of opposing political forces to do this. The right and the left of politics let each other off the hook: by declining to reform the banks thoroughly and introduce new regulations to restrict dangerous trading instruments such as CDOs, conservatives hand a gift to the left. And by refusing to give more than token respect to the need for fiscal responsibility, the left make it easy for their opponents. It is a blame game in which those really to blame escape accountability. The extreme and unethical nature of neo-liberalism has probably hindered the modernisation of trade unions towards a more partnership role: it is harder to sell the case of partnership deals when the dominant business model is hostile to the worker's interests. At many more enlightened organisations, of course, the model is ignored and sensible deals are struck.

There may be an element of collective amnesia, also, in our responses to crisis, or simply a case of being daunted by the scale of the challenge. In the aftermath

---

1   Quoted by Jeremy Warner: Does anyone seriously think another VAT cut will cure the economy? *The Telegraph*, 23 May 2012. Available at: http://www.telegraph.co.uk/ finance/comment/jeremy-warner/9286255/Does-anyone-honestly-think-another-VAT -cut-would-cure-economy.html [accessed 28 October 2012]. Full essay at: The True Lessons of the Recession, Raghuram Rajan, *Foreign Affairs*, May/June 2012. Available at: http:// www.foreignaffairs.com/articles/134863/raghuram-g-rajan/the-true-lessons-of-the-recession [accessed 28 October 2012].

of the first wave of the credit crisis, 2007–2010, there were TV documentaries, political speeches and proposals related to remedying the broken business model, understanding better the dynamics of credit boom and investment bubbles and the failed policies that contributed. These initiatives seem to have petered out. Our short-termist political/economic leadership seems incapable of rising to the challenge.

Nowhere is the complacent return to 'business as usual' more evident than at JP Morgan Bank, which became the largest in the US after the adjustments and consolidation following Lehman Brothers' collapse in 2008. The bank's CEO Jamie Dimon has led the political campaign against more regulation, including on proprietary trading. In April 2012, asked about potential losses in London trades, he described this as a 'tempest in a teacup'. Just one month later he had to confess to an unexpected $2bn trading loss from the London branch of its Chief Investment Office. Nominally, the office was operating sensible hedging operations, but more critical observers conclude that it was effectively engaging in high-risk proprietary trading,[2] taking on risks it could not calculate or handle, in a disturbing repeat of many of the features of the CDO scandal of the previous decade.

The ability of banks to police themselves still appears to rest upon hubristic ambition, rather than cool-headed understanding of the risks incurred. Any attempt to dazzle the public with technocratic language struggles as we begin to discern that the emperor is wearing no clothes. Many politicians, however, are still admiring the stitching.

THE GOVERNMENT IS NOT THE ECONOMY

The government is not the economy. The economy is not money. The economy is people and organisations. Money is just a by-product of what people and organisations do, and the government is just one of the organisations in the economy.

For many commentators, and far too many economists, the government 'is' the economy. People clamour for 'growth', which they wrongly assume is an increase in GDP measured on a quarterly basis. For all the reasons discussed in Chapter 1, this is misleading and can lead to policies that undermine genuine, sustainable growth. By not even recording basic liabilities such as government debt or trading deficits, GDP figures can be dangerously misleading. At a very minimum, their publication should be accompanied by a range of supplementary data on public sector liabilities, trading position, patent development, start-up success rates, university rankings, educational standards and so on. For an intelligent discussion of the options, we

---

2   Press reports, for example, JP Morgan $2bn loss: Dimon's in the rough, *The Telegraph*, 11 May 2012; also JP Morgan's Dimon: Losing trades were an isolated event, CNN Money, 21 May 2012.

would recommend *The Economics of Enough*, by economist Diane Coyle, in which she argues for a rounded measure of economic growth, rather than the two-dimensional headline of changes in GDP.[3]

There is a similar bias within business, where debt is often treated more favourably than other forms of investment from a tax point of view, and where 'leverage' has been used to finance overambitious private equity deals, repeating the over-optimistic projections of governments and investment banks. All these institutional biases towards consumption and 'growth' today, financed by taxes on our children, have to be challenged and reversed.

Business-people clamouring for a 'growth strategy' from government is a bit like a footballer blaming his lack of goals on the chairman of the national Football Association. Obviously, where a government is guilty of corruption, mismanagement, unreasonable bureaucratic burdens or excessive taxes, business leaders must speak out. But as for 'growth'; this comes more from business themselves than from ministers. The best thing that governments can do is create skilled people and uphold the law, including civil law. Nationalising the growth strategies can become a self-fulfilling prophesy, in which individuals, NGOs, businesses, communities and so on passively assume a mythical 'pyramid' shape to the economy, with national government at the apex, responsible for all growth and all activity, and to be held to blame for everything that goes wrong. Apart from anything else, in an open-trading, globalised world, such a view is an anachronism as well as an abdication of responsibility. Worse, it encourages governments to pursue the illusion of 'growth' as measured by GDP increases, through public debt-fuelled activity – policies that ended in disaster in Greece (see Chapter 6).

NEW LEADERSHIP, UNEXPECTED SOURCES

Such are the headlines. What we have discovered in years of work with leading business-people is that the more enlightened businesses are exhibiting real leadership that creates growth that can be sustained beyond a few quarters of financial reporting. John Mackey, co-founder of Whole Foods, simply ignores the superficial economic arguments in the papers, sees through the incoherence of left-wing and right-wing economic theories that pretend the world consists of 'systems' or that the company is like a machine, and proceeds to run his firm on the basis that pleasing the customer, creating careers for his workers and protecting the environment, makes business, social and economic sense. He writes of the 'paradox of profit', the phenomenon in which exclusive focus upon profit maximisation does not result in maximum profits – for many reasons, including the misunderstanding of the importance of

---

3   Coyle, Diane, *The Economics of Enough: How to Run the Economy as if the Future Matters*, Princeton University Press, 2011.

interdependence and trust in making a business work. A successful entrepreneur is more like a creative artist (our summary, not Mackey's term). He writes: 'I have known many entrepreneurs in my life, and with only a few exceptions most did not create their business primarily to maximise profits'.[4]

Another example of social innovation that breaks with the cynicism of economic theory is Grameen Bank in Bangladesh, founded by Professor Muhammad Yunus, which has liberated thousands of people from poverty through its ingenious micro-finance facilities for entrepreneurs.[5] Semco, led and reinvented by Ricardo Semler, is one of the more celebrated examples of enlightened leadership. Note how, on the website, the principles of inclusiveness, balance between long and short-term success, and ethical conduct are described as 'unconventional', at times almost with an apologetic air.[6]

Umair Haque, author and blogger, has published his *The New Capitalist Manifesto*, describing the financial crisis as really just a by-product of an ethical crisis. The *Harvard Business Review* notes:

> *It's a crisis of institutions and ideals inherited from the industrial age. These ideals include rampant exploitation of resources, top-down command of resource allocations, withholding of information from stakeholders to control them, and a single-minded pursuit of profit for its own sake. All this has produced 'thin value' short-term economic gains that accrue to some people far more than others, and that don't make us happier or healthier.*

In *The New Capitalist Manifesto*, Haque describes:

- Renewal: use resources sustainably to maximise efficiencies.
- Democracy: allocate resources democratically to foster organisational agility.
- Peace: practice economic non-violence in business.
- Equity: create industries that make the least well off better off.
- Meaning: generate payoffs that tangibly improve quality of life.[7]

---

4   Conscious capitalism: creating a new paradigm for business, John Mackey blog, 9 November 2006. Available at: http://www2.wholefoodsmarket.com/blogs/jmackey/2006/11/09/conscious-capitalism-creating-a-new-paradigm-for-business/ [accessed 13 June 2012].
5   A Short History of Grameen Bank. Available at: http://www.grameen-info.org/index.php?option=com_content&task=view&id=19&Itemid=114 [accessed 28 October 2012].
6   The Semco Way, Semco website. Available at: http://www.semco.com.br/en/content.asp?content=3&contentID=566 [accessed 28 October 2012].
7   *The New Capitalist Manifesto*, Umair Haque, Harvard Business Review Books, 4 January 2011. Available at: http://hbr.org/product/baynote/an/12794-HBK-ENG?referral=00506 [accessed 13 June 2012].

Again, as discussed in Chapter 4 (subsection 'Are Business-people the New Progressives?') we would challenge the view that the Manifesto described above, and indeed by ourselves, is wholly new, as there are some echoes of ideas by Deming, Parker-Follett and others in the early to mid-twentieth century. We need to develop an understanding of why we haven't learned these lessons before, to help ensure we learn them properly this time. Our conclusion is that the explanation for their failure to flourish is the toxic influence of political–economic theories of both left and right, which is why we have devoted so much space to them in this book.

The sort of intellectual leadership that ought to come from the political left now comes from within business: moral outrage at inequality, exploitation and ecological degradation, backed not by nationalist–populist policies that will sow envy, division and further inequality and waste; but enlightened principles that will create jobs through participative, responsible businesses, increasing living standards and enhancing environmental protection.

Another glimmer of leadership in the fog of mediocrity is Andrew Haldane, executive director financial stability at the Bank of England. In a lecture in October 2011 he described widening inequalities, undeserved executive pay and described how the serious imbalance between privatised returns and socialised risks 'calls for fundamental reform'.[8] In summer 2012 he renewed his criticism, denouncing calculus-based models widely used by investment banks that had failed to anticipate catastrophic risk, and calling again for 'a fairly fundamental re-think of the foundations of modern-day economics, finance and econometrics'.[9]

Picking up similar themes, Liam Halligan of the UK-based *The Sunday Telegraph* deserves mention for highlighting the centrality of the banks, and their lobbying, as principal causes of the crisis. The left/right positing of economic choice as one of 'growth versus austerity' is meaningless, he argues. The real problem is the zombie banks, the refusal of their leaders fully to reveal their losses, in part because of the impact on their remuneration, and the timidity of politicians in confronting the banking lobby.[10]

---

8   Wincott Annual Memorial Lecture, Andrew Haldane, Westminster London, 24 October 2011. Full text available at: http://www.bankofengland.co.uk/publications/Documents/speeches/2011/speech525.pdf [accessed 11 June 2012].
9   Paper to University of Edinburgh Business School. See press report: Risk models must be torn up, says Haldane, *The Telegraph*, 8 June 2012. Available at: http://www.telegraph.co.uk/finance/economics/9319127/Risk-models-must-be-torn-up-Haldane-says.html [accessed 11 June 2012].
10   Regular column. See, for example: UK and Europe languish in a 'zombie bank' malaise, *The Sunday Telegraph*, 9 June 2012. Available at: http://www.telegraph.co.uk/finance/comment/liamhalligan/9321796/UK-and-Europe-languish-in-a-zombie-bank-malaise.html [accessed 11 June 2012].

SOCIAL RIGHTS VERSUS ECONOMIC RIGHTS

It is universally accepted among liberal and centre-left thinkers and trade unionists that all social and economic benefits must come as 'of right', rather than be dependent upon the whim or charity of a wealthy individual or agency. There is little discussion of the distinction between constitutional or social rights versus economic rights, and it is taboo in many circles to question the established assumptions. Yet there is a significant difference between social entitlement, such as the right to freedom from discrimination or to a fair trial, and the 'right' to an economic benefit that has an impact on others – such as job security, retirement age or defined pension benefits. Economic rights always come with economic costs. These may be minor and dispersed widely, or fall largely upon very wealthy people, in which cases the concern is minor. But in an increasingly interdependent and over-indebted world, this is less and less the case.

Is it really 'progressive' for healthy and wealthy 61-year-old retired European civil servants, enjoying life in their second homes, to be subsidised by hard-working, lower paid people? And to be enjoying such leisure at the public expense not for a few years, but for a few decades, with the full cost passed on to their children and grandchildren, who face little prospect of enjoying such benefits, and who face working longer to cope with those debts? This is not a hypothetical scenario: Uruguay by the end of the twentieth century presented an example of a country with arguably the longest-established welfare state in the world, and all manner of economic 'rights', but too little money in the economy for such entitlements to be of any real merit.[11] Such a prospect now faces much of Europe.

There is a similarly misplaced emphasis upon rights, rather than economic opportunity, for those of working age. Whenever a government recommends deregulatory measures in the European labour market – the *reforma laboral* in Spain, or the Beecroft Report in the UK, both proposed in 2012 – there are howls of protest from the left that this leaves workers vulnerable. In the British Parliament on 21 May 2012, the Liberal Democrat Lorely Burt said that proposals to make it easier to dismiss staff would create 'a climate of fear', and the Labour MP David Crausby asked how it would help to make workers 'terrified' of losing their jobs,[12] while his boss, the Labour leader Ed Miliband said at Prime Minister's Question Time in the House of Commons, and we quote in full: 'Some people will be dismissed simply because their employer doesn't like them'.

Such sentiments pass almost without comment, yet deserve scrutiny. Where do these beliefs come from, that fear helps the business, and can only be prevented by

---

11   Observations and conclusions from a study tour of social care and the welfare state in Uruguay in 1991 by Philip Whiteley.
12   Hansard, 21 May 2012.

legislation? How can a climate of fear help win orders and please customers? Is it really the case that the only factor deterring business leaders from instituting private tyrannies is the presence of legislation?

While enlightened leadership does not consist only of encouragement; there has to be accountability and discipline as well (see Chapter 7), a prolonged atmosphere of fear and distrust is as damaging for profit margins as it is for collective self-esteem. This is well established in management literature, supported by a considerable amount of evidence over the past 20 years, by such academics as Jeffrey Pfeffer and Daniel Goleman; and longer still, if one includes the empirical evidence of organisations that followed the advice of W Edwards Deming to 'banish fear' from the workplace and to support teamwork. The findings of Elton Mayo in the Hawthorne experiments in the 1930s came to similar conclusions, but were not widely implemented. To be more precise, the research indicates that fear can be legitimately used for very short periods, at times of crisis where a workforce has become complacent, but that it is ruinous for companies over the longer term.[13]

Of course there are plenty of managers in corporations who operate entirely on fear. Such ogres do not only feature in corporations, but can also be encountered in government agencies, NGOs, political parties and trade unions – a factor rarely admitted in political debate. What is not at all established, or supported by the evidence base, is the organisational benefit that fear brings, other than the specific and rare context referred to. But one reason for highlighting the political comments above is to warn of the risk of the self-fulfilling prophesy. Centuries of Marxists and neo-liberals claiming that exploitation is the way to boost margins, encourages the worst types of managerial style to be deployed. Employee relations can descend into a self-fulfilling, vicious cycle of mutual fear and threat, with management and unions seeing themselves as being on opposite sides of a conflict, each keen to get their retaliation in first. This unhealthy dynamic was the principal cause of the collapse of entire industries in some western countries in the 1970s and 1980s, and was largely self-fulfilling, based on inaccurate and cynical political philosophies.

These Parliamentary statements illustrate how deeply ingrained the hyper-cynicism of neo-liberal/Marxist assumptions remain in the political subconscious. They also display a disturbing ignorance of how the working world actually functions. Now it may be the case that politicians maintain a climate of fear for their own staff, but that is a problem for them to sort out – such an approach doesn't work in the world

---

13   Pfeffer, Jeffrey, *The Human Equation: Building Profits by Putting People First*, Harvard Business Press, 1998; Pfeffer, Jeffrey and Sutton, Robert, *Hard Facts, Dangerous Half-Truths and Total Nonsense: Profiting from Evidence-Based Management*, Harvard Business School Press, 2006; Goleman, Daniel, *Emotional Intelligence*, Bloomsbury, 1996; Whiteley, Philip and Bloch, Susan, *Complete Leadership*, Pearson, 2003.

of business. There is similar cynicism and ignorance in the trade unions and political parties across much of Europe, especially France and Spain.

The exception has been Germany, where a social contract was established in the early 2000s between workers and managers to exchange higher productivity and wage restraint in return for employment creation and job security. It is no coincidence that Germany is the strongest economy in Europe, with the lowest unemployment and the strongest exports. Yet still political leaders in many countries pretend that economic performance depends upon demand management, rather than business leadership. At the point of writing, a common complaint of Germany is that it is 'too successful', and needs to introduce more inefficiency and inflationary wage settlements in order to help the single European currency survive. Perhaps the same principle could be extended to football, so that Germany doesn't win so many games. The side could take the field with only eight players, perhaps.

Rather than improve the weaker economies, the EU's leaders plan, at the time of writing, to make the strongest economy less successful. And then borrow more than the productive base can withstand. When politicians start to parody themselves, we are well on the way to decline.

By definition, a demand or entitlement is unconditional: it undermines any notion of reciprocity. That is its whole point. One of the most baleful consequences of the culture of entitlement has been to chip away at the concepts of mutuality and community that had been one of the founding principles of the socialist and cooperative movements in the nineteenth century. While the cult of entitlement, and entitlement spending by the state, has grown considerably over the past two decades, there was little or no organised opposition to the destruction of mutual societies in the UK, for example, a disastrous policy which, combined with the cult of short-termism in banking, the financial markets and company management generally, contributed to the credit crisis and consequent economic recession. In terms of rhetoric, the entitlement culture and neo-liberalism are distinct from one another, but behaviourally there is a strong similarity, a case of saying: 'Give me my rewards now; the impact on other stakeholders doesn't concern me'.

Having said that, the claims for enterprising effects of deregulation of working conditions by right-wing economists tend to be exaggerated. As discussed at the beginning of Chapter 3, from right-wing economic institutes there is a lop-sided emphasis on 'labour market reform' in many economic programmes, and insufficient attention to skills development and management reform. Some economies with relatively high levels of labour regulation, such as Sweden, are still able to generate jobs and high-quality business clusters.

Adrian Beecroft, author of the controversial report referred to recommending deregulatory changes, claimed that implementing all his ideas would add 5 per cent to GDP.[14] This looks like a doubtful claim, especially in a country where it is likely that skills shortages are the bigger problem than bureaucratic difficulties with hiring and firing. In one survey, four out of ten business leaders described themselves unhappy with the levels of literacy of school leavers; 35 per cent expressed concern over numeracy.[15] In addition around one in five young people are not in education, employment or training.[16] There is a huge opportunity cost when low skills are so widespread: the businesses that are not set up; the hirer who gives up after interviewing 20 people and instead contracts the work in another country or tries to get by without, hampering business growth and limiting international expansion.

Economic and business development is a multi-dimensional dynamic, ideally featuring strong skills, entrepreneurial endeavour, strong management abilities, access to capital, leading research at universities, low corruption levels, a good infrastructure and robust contract law. The degree of bureaucracy involved relating to regulations intended to provide certain protections for workers should be optimal rather than maximised. Their absence does not automatically imply tyranny for the workers or hyper-growth for the capitalist; it is actually one of the more minor factors at play, unless they are extremely high or low. The fact that proposals to alter such laws to even a small degree generate such considerable political heat illustrates the depressing extent to which simplistic economic theories of left and right continue to hold sway, and distract us from more important matters that underpin economic development.

SHORT-TERMISM IS HOLDING BACK PROGRESS

The response of many European prime ministers and presidents in the depth of the eurozone crisis – to make the strongest economies weaker and to add more borrowing requirements on to an already indebted continent – appear doomed to failure. They are not so much a failure of 'left' or of 'right' but of short-termism; by governments, banks, venture capitalists, economists – Keynesians or Friedmanites – alike.

This is now holding up progress, for example in new energy-smart technologies. There is a wealth of promising research in zero-carbon technologies that is being held up because impatient investors want a quicker return.

---

14   'Socialist' Vince Cable not fit for office, says Adrian Beecroft, *The Telegraph*, 23 May 2012.
15   School leavers lacking basic skills, bosses group says, BBC News, 9 May 2011. Available at: http://www.bbc.co.uk/news/education-13310246 [accessed 23 May 2012].
16   Record number of young unemployed Neets, *The Telegraph*, 24 November 2011. Available at: http://www.telegraph.co.uk/education/8911996/Record-number-of-young-unemployed-Neets.html [accessed 28 October 2012].

The sectarianism of the climate wars does not help (see Chapter 1). By placing all their eggs in the 'climate change' basket, campaigners are vulnerable should they make even minor errors or exaggerations. By ignoring the multitude of economic benefits of reduced fossil fuel usage, climate sceptics are passing over some massive opportunities that could have as big an impact on business performance and efficiency and economic growth as the industrial revolution two centuries ago.

Some types of green technology, such as tidal power for generating electricity, have been available since the 1960s, yet still lack significant investment, because gas and oil have been convenient in the short term. The problem with that strategy is that the short term is now over. If environmental considerations are not a high enough priority, surely petrol (gas) prices should be. The price at the pump has become a major political controversy, especially in the USA and India. In May 2012, India's opposition parties called for a national strike to protest against pump prices,[17] and the same issue emerged as a key source of controversy in the US Presidential election in the same year; it has also prompted a significant expansion of controversial shale gas exploration, following restrictions on deep-water drilling after the 2010 BP Gulf of Mexico disaster.

A valuable description of the growth of short-termism in investment circles, and how it has been encouraged and reflected in changes to company structure and many jurisdictions in the west, can be found in Gordon Pearson's *The Road to Co-operation*.[18] Contrasting the original concept of enlightened self-interest of Adam Smith with the more recent crude distortion of 'maximising shareholder value', Pearson points out that the original intention of capital-raising in the capitalist system has been completely inverted. Practices such as the widening of share and bond ownership and limited liability in the industrial revolution facilitated raising of substantial investments to fund major infrastructure programmes, initially the canals and the turnpike roads in the UK. These were long-term projects; investors accepted it would be nearly a decade before a return would be seen. Over the years since, and especially in recent decades, the emphasis is inverted: instead of raising capital for worthwhile projects, enterprises are seen as vehicles for the benefit of capital. 'Value' in the phrase 'maximising shareholder value' means maximum short-term returns for transient investors with little real lasting stake in the success or otherwise of the project. Both Pearson and Bob Garratt (*Fish Rots from the Head*, and *Thin on Top*)[19]

---

17   India opposition calls for nationwide strike to protest rising petrol price, *International Business Times*, 24 May 2012.

18   Pearson, Gordon, *The Road to Co-operation: Escaping the Bottom Line*, Gower Publishing, 2012.

19   Garratt, Bob and Brealey, Nicholas, *Thin on Top: Why Corporate Governance Matters* and *How to Measure and Improve Board Performance*, 2003. Garratt, Bob, *The Fish Rots from the Head: The Crisis in Our Boardrooms – Developing the Crucial Skills of the Competent Director*, Profile Books, 3rd revised edition, 2010.

point out that this speculative cult has also had the effect of undermining company law, in which the directors' principle of stewardship of the company has been a duty frequently honoured in the breach rather than the observance (see Chapter 3).

Changes to the ownership structures have served to weaken still further the links between investor and enterprise, and encourage dangerous speculation and short-termism. The rise of the 'limited liability partnership' made it safer for investors to take investment risks – safer for themselves that is; in practice costs of excessively risky trades are externalised and, of course, since the collapse of Lehman Brothers but rescue of other institutions, the cost has been passed on to taxpayers. Similarly, many investment banks reconstituted themselves as plcs in the 1990s, and the Clinton administration followed the UK's big bang of 1986 with repeal of Glass-Steagall.

The neo-classical faith in self-regulating markets has now been demonstrated as a misguided theology – by an increasing number in the financial markets themselves. The toxic effect of neo-classical, or neo-liberal ideas on management is still with us, however.

SURPLUS VALUE AND THE IRON LAW OF WAGES

The Marxist theory is that the capitalist steals the worker's time: for only a few minutes of each hour is the worker working for himself; the value that is surplus to this goes into the hands of the greedy capitalist, who seeks to maximise it. Here we see a direct similarity between Marxism and the neo-liberal cult of maximisation of recent years.

Surplus value is essentially the same as the 'law of the irreducible minimum' or iron law of wages, popularised in the nineteenth century.[20] Economists such as David Ricardo and the classical economists described this supposed 'iron' law as being one that determined that employers will logically pay workers no more than the basic minimum necessary for subsistence. Such theorists tended to refer to labour in terms of 'supply', as if people were aggregates, without the tiniest acknowledgement of matters such as skills, morale, teamwork and productivity, and ignoring the empirical evidence that the more principled Quaker businesses of the day, blithely ignoring such 'laws' and treating their workers better than average, tended to be more commercially successful than others. There is a deeply unscientific assumption

---

20   See http://en.wikipedia.org/wiki/Iron_law_of_wages [accessed 5 November 2012]. The same principle was discussed in the influential novel *Germinal*, by Emile Zola, described as the 'law of the irreducible minimum' in the Penguin English translation. In this edition, the footnotes indicate that Zola's source was probably *Le Socialisme Contemporain* by E. de Laveleye. Philip Whiteley discussed the impact of literature on attitudes to management in the e-book *Meet the New Boss*, self-published on Kindle, 2010.

at play in 'scientific' economists. A proper engineer will be well schooled in the discipline of materials science; the economist, by contrast, shows a misanthropic disinclination to understand or study human behaviour.

As critiqued by Philip Whiteley and Max Mckeown a decade ago:

> *To begin with, it [Marx's theory of surplus value] ignores the passage of time. This matters in a number of ways; the future value of the learning that the worker may be gaining in her hour of working can be considerable; and this might more than outweigh the apparent losses by working for most of the hour for someone else. The surplus value calculation takes the worker and boss as being curiously isolated from the rest of the world. There is no notion of inter-dependence; that the proprietor gives as well as takes; that he or she is a worker too.*[21]

Such crude theories have gained the lustre of academic respectability through the adoption of an entire lexicon of euphemisms on the left, and unsafe but complex-looking calculus equations on the right.

Surplus value and the 'iron law' are without foundation, and have been comprehensively undermined by studies into actual organisational behaviour from the 1930s to the present day by researchers such as Elton Mayo, Jeffrey Pfeffer and Lynda Gratton (see Chapter 3). To our knowledge, the findings of such research have not been used to challenge the diametric opposite view still put forward by right-wing and left-wing economic theories. Again, we see an introduction of the concept of a 'law' akin to the material sciences, unsupported by any evidence, illogical in its application to societies of sentient beings, undermined by even the most cursory observations in a real workplace, and highly damaging to people and organisations in attempts to use them to inform management and economic stewardship.

The value added by the engagement and skill of employees nearly always vastly outweighs the direct costs of hire. Moreover, this applies in so-called low-wage, low-skill industries as well as areas such as hi-tech research where there may be fierce competition for the most able individuals and it is perhaps more obvious that engagement and the career offering are of competitive advantage. This is one reason why we have sought to highlight case studies such as Bangladeshi textile workers employed by providers for Marks & Spencer, and ancillary staff at the office services provider ISS, illustrating that the principles of enlightened leadership and better profits from better treatment of staff, apply universally.

People at all levels in society don't only want protection and entitlements; nor simply 'jobs'. People also want careers, some sense of achievement and pride in working

---

21   McKeown, Max and Whiteley, Philip, *Unshrink: Yourself, Other People, Business, the World*, Pearson, 2002.

for an employer that provides a good service and is well regarded. In the real world, this is a more lasting kind of job security than the one promised in legislation in a bureaucratic state where the real unemployment rate is 20–30 per cent. This is a universal desire. The most important person in an employee's life is his or her boss, not the employment minister, the tribunal chair or the head of the Supreme Court. Political initiatives in the workplace ought to be diverted wholesale towards encouraging the good boss, rather than providing highly imperfect remedies for bad ones.

This little trip into nineteenth-century economic thought is not merely for historical background. Our experience has led us to conclude that belief in the core assumption of the 'iron law' or surplus value theory is still widespread, despite evidence that it can almost never be observed in practice. It continues to disfigure our understanding of the role of business and management, the drafting of employee legislation and priorities in government policy relating to the workplace. It has been absorbed into the collective subconscious, like water in porous rock, seeping out at meetings of finance managers, Occupy protest chants and Prime Minister's Question Time. If many business leaders, MBA course lecturers, free-market economists, and nearly all trade union leaders and left-wing politicians *believe*, deep-down, that minimising the wage bill maximises profits, it is hardly surprising that there are a lot of low wages, causing damage to household incomes, local communities and businesses themselves.

It is a hard-wired belief of many business planners, who make outsourcing decisions on the basis of the direct cost of employment, taking insufficient account of the value added. Often such costly and disruptive restructures have to be reversed a few years later. Belief in the iron law can also be witnessed in workplace rights campaigners. In 2011, the New York-based China Labor Watch published a damning report on working conditions in many supplier companies for major US corporations such as Apple. It contained the following paragraph:

> *Foxconn should not bear the only responsibility for worker suicides: Apple, HP, Dell and other international OEMs should also be held responsible, as their goal of profit maximisation comes at the cost of workers' wages and sub-optimal working conditions.*[22]

This displays faith in the commercial logic of exploitation, and belief that only the shame of publicity or the force of law can prevent rational managers from pursuing this path. The chronicling of poor conditions was indeed shocking, yet there was scant recognition that this can generate operational risk, as well as miserable lives

---

22   Tragedies of globalization: the truth behind electronics sweatshops, report by China Labor Watch, July 2011. Available at: http://chinalaborwatch.org/news/new-350.html [accessed 28 October 2012].

for the workers. Belief in the 'iron law' – a product of right-wing classical economic thought – appears absolute among left-wing employee rights campaigners. In a newspaper report on the scandal of worker suicides and related matters, a response to the China Labor Watch report, attributed to the one of the suppliers Tyco: 'We have a high turnover rate of workers in this industry' (*Daily Telegraph*, 21 July 2011).

This is highly revealing. Research on the business impact of staff turnover shows that managers routinely underestimate its cost, and that many initiatives to reduce this save the company money, typically outweighing the cost of increased wages and training opportunities. To our knowledge the most comprehensive analysis of this approach, illustrated by company case studies, is the 2003 work *Play to Your Strengths*, by Haig Nalbantian, Richard Guzzo, David Kieffer and Jay Doherty.[23]

This does not mean that all workplace regulations can safely be dispensed with. It is a question of balance. For the past 20 years or so in the west, regulations have been steadily increased for enterprising companies seeking to provide socially useful goods and services, yet successively removed for speculative activities such as trading in securitised mortgage products that no one understands. We need a rebalancing.

THE ECONOMY IS NOT A SYSTEM

A tacit shared assumption of left and right is that the economy is an inanimate, mechanistic machine, in some unexplained way separate from the people and organisations that actually comprise a real society. There has been a common, if not perhaps quite universal, belief in mechanistic forces that economies are supposed to follow. This has been widely believed since the so-called 'Enlightenment'; it appears, for example that the *Rights of Man* author Thomas Paine believed that economic forces could be codified and explained through laws similar to Newton's laws governing planetary motion and human-made machines.[24]

Marxist textbooks assume the same *a priori* belief; that 'capitalism' and 'socialism' are systems that obey historic forces explained by secret esoteric formulae that only professors can understand. In a similar way, entire risk models in the investment banking system also assumed the kind of random statistical variation that one might expect in a closed game of chance with a finite set of variables – a belief system comprehensively rebutted by Nassim Nicholas Taleb, who pointed also to the absurd assumption of Darwinist forces at play in the way in which organisations perform were supposed to improve themselves endlessly amid the fierce competition of

---

23   Nalbantian, Haig, Guzzo, Richard, Kieffer, David and Doherty, Jay, *Play to Your Strengths*, McGraw-Hill, 2003.
24   Keane, John, *Thomas Paine: A Political Life*, Bloomsbury, 1996.

the marketplace and the quarterly report. 'In practice, it isn't as simple as that', he explains with uncharacteristic understatement.[25]

One of the problems with assuming competing economic 'systems', mysteriously unoccupied by sentient human beings, overlaid by left/right sectarianism, is that it makes it difficult to identify similar patterns of behaviour operating in differently constituted organisations. Business groups will denounce waste in government spending projects, while overlooking waste from misjudgements and poor planning in mergers and acquisitions. Trade unionists will denounce neglectful care in privately-run hospitals but often show less concern over deaths through neglect in public sector hospitals[26].

A behavioural understanding of economics and management challenges long-held beliefs of left and of right. Exploitative management is behavioural; it isn't caused by the profit motive. Efficient operation is the result of effective leadership, not an inevitable by-product of competition. The structure and form of ownership are assumed by left and right-wing thinkers to largely determine how an organisation performs, but in the real world they are minor contributory factors, compared with the values and conduct of the leadership team and the skills and motivation of the employee population generally.

The ultimate irony is that even the material world may not obey 'laws'; or rather that these laws may be temporary and only approximately correct, according to many leading physicists. The inability of human-invented scientific laws to describe the universe is causing a major crisis in physics, and the dawn of a heretical idea that, perhaps, scientific laws are descriptive and approximate, not definitive and precise. Biologist Rupert Sheldrake, for example, suggests that laws do not hold in the biological space; also that they may evolve – after all, life does.[27]

In management and economics, the irony is that a belief in 'laws' under the guise of scientific management or classical economics, has actually undermined the proper discipline of science, which is accurate observation and an understanding of the context and the evidence base. If we dispense with imaginary laws and the spurious formulae of Marxism and neo-liberalism, we are left with observation. In our experience, the only two safe operating assumptions about organisational management and economics are the following:

---

25   Taleb, Nassim Nicholas, *The Black Swan: the Impact of the Highly Improbable*, Random House, 2007. Also recommended: *Fooled by Randomness*, by the same author, Penguin reissue, 2007.

26   There has been little public protest or discussion in the UK over the deaths through neglect at the Mid-Staffordshire NHS Hospital. See inquiry website: http://www. midstaffspublicinquiry.com/ [accessed 12 November 2012].

27   Sheldrake, Rupert, *The Science Delusion*, Coronet, 2012.

1. The economy consists of people.
2. People behave like people.

The tautology is deliberate and bears repeating. Most of the economic and managerial disasters of the past few decades; in both the public and private sector, influenced by right and left-wing theories alike, stem from ignoring these basic operating principles.

The bias is seen in economic policy-setting and company reporting. It is even observable in the way in which conventional newspapers and news websites are configured, in which 'Finance' sits at the top, with 'Business' below that, and 'Management' a small and often occasional subset below that. This is precisely the opposite of how organisations and economies actually function, and the reverse order of importance.

It is worth recapping the extent to which the dominant economic ideologies of the modern age have failed, the extent to which they have poisoned management theory, and the lack of endeavour in producing coherent alternatives that are based on how people actually live their lives. According to Marxist doctrine, the free-market 'system' should not have proved more durable than the Soviet system. According to neo-liberal doctrine, deregulated financial markets should have been automatically stabilising; the Lehman Brothers collapse should never have happened, and Enron represented a far more dynamic and enterprising business model than Whole Foods. The events of autumn 2008 were every bit as devastating for neo-liberal, Friedmanite thoughts and assumptions as the collapse of the Berlin Wall was for the idea of an international alternative to capitalism.

Unfortunately, there is now an ideological vacuum. Instead of replacing Marxism and neo-liberalism, economists and politicians pretend that we can get by without any ideology. The result is continued, frenetic opportunism and populist initiatives, in which the ideas of the past, failed ideologies resurface from the collective subconscious.

ARBITRARY SEPARATION

Closely linked to the pseudo-science of pretending that the economy is an inanimate system, and that the company is a machine, is the arbitrary and damaging separation of organisational theory from politics and from economic theory. At work are the assumptions that the economy does not consist of people; that findings from leadership studies should not influence political leadership; that practice should be divorced from theory, that political ideas can be free of ideology.

This is related to the unfortunate separation of philosophy from science during the Enlightenment. Compounding this was the pretence that economics could be treated as a science akin to the material sciences, rather than a form of applied anthropology.

In management literature, theoretical books and practical books are produced and categorised separately. A central theme of this book is to bring the two together: conscious leadership means understanding, engaging with, and sometimes challenging one's core beliefs about the world and the organisation, and the internalised 'scripts' that each leader has (see Chapter 7). Ideology affects behaviour. In the same way the development of ideas and ideology are linked to culture, personal background and development. Personality affects ideology.

Another by-product of this separation is that even within more enlightened circles, the big picture often becomes lost. There are earnest, esoteric debates on the merits of different approaches to social responsibility: is CSR better than CSV, and so on, that have a worrying resemblance to MBA theories where arbitrary social concepts are assumed to be tangible and universally understood. In human capital circles, there are frequently intense debates on the distinction between correlation and cause and effect on a matter such as employee engagement. Too often, these discussions end up like the theological debates over the number of angels that can dance on the head of a pin. The broader, empirical findings of leadership and organisation imply such a huge change from the taken-for-granted notions of the twentieth century that any significant step towards enacting them should be welcomed as progress, not analysed to death by new forms of bean-counting. Worse, there can be a tendency to hold back on promising new developments until they can be made perfect. In the human capital world in particular, there is a misplaced onus on new systems to prove their worth beyond reasonable doubt, based on the misleading assumption that any alternative must be better in the absence of such proof – another example of the 'binary delusion'. It is almost as though there is a residual belief in the 'iron law' of wages, in the pursuit of profit maximisation through exploitation, even in adherents of human capital management and social responsibility. Many can be harsher on their peers in those disciplines than on proponents of finance-based management, appearing to lack faith in the conclusions of their own research.

In pretty much any organisation, an employee engagement measure is a step forward. Of course the results of employee opinion surveys may be misinterpreted or over-interpreted; but that is true of any source of data or intelligence in management. In some circumstances employee engagement scores may be well interpreted but still inadequate to deal with seismic market changes; they can never be a guarantor of commercial success. But such information is still better than complete ignorance of your workforce, which was the twentieth century operating model, and remains the default option for those not daring to move forward, however imperfectly.

It is still rare to seriously consider one's own ideology; to why we do things and on what basis; to linking an understanding of our beliefs, values and thoughts; our 'way of being' to conduct and decisions, in line with the principles of conscious leadership discussed in Chapter 7. Many employee rights campaigners assume that the social dumping argument is consistent with the theory of engaged employees; the MBA course tacitly assumes that cost-based outsourcing is consistent with engagement. On neither side is there awareness of the inconsistency, nor is there serious enquiry when matters go wrong. In mergers and outsourcing, for example, many post-mortems blame 'cultural differences' for their failure. Yet rarely is 'cultural fit' considered in the due-diligence phase, nor contingency planning for ensuring that such typically ambitious business plans have the best chance of succeeding. Even where there is much work to secure a shared vision and culture fit, for example at the successful cross-border joint venture Sony-Ericsson,[28] one struggles to find recognition of this in the business pages, where the human causes of business success get translated into the opaque language of finance.

IN SUMMARY

The failure of neo-liberal, right-wing economic theory and its damaging business model raises the risk that it will be replaced by some equally damaging populist approaches. The fact that an approach is stridently different does not automatically make it better. The radical shift that is really needed is an understanding of the behavioural nature of economics, and a break with the short-termism of both left and right-wing economics.

---

28   See interview with Miles Flint, then President Sony-Ericsson, in Bloch, Susan and Whiteley, Philip, *How to Manage in a Flat World*, Pearson, 2007.

CHAPTER 9

FROM SUPPLY CHAIN TO SUPPLY CIRCLE

There have been many comparisons made recently between the current crisis and the banking and financial crisis of the late 1920s, followed by the depression of the 1930s. There is a huge difference, however, and that is the rise in population, living standards and spread of industrialisation to regions that were previously characterised by subsistence farming. George Orwell was able to state, in the 1937 publication *The Road to Wigan Pier*,[1] that the world has 'plenty of provisions for everybody', how a fairer system for their distribution had a natural appeal, but that there were no real concerns over supply. This can no longer be assumed to be the case.

Business has to lie at the heart of any change that acknowledges this fundamental shift; one that has been described by Bob Willard, as discussed in Chapter 7, as a move from 'take–make–waste' to the sustainable practice of 'borrow–use–return'.[2] Another writer on the subject, John Elkington, pithily says: 'It's about how we shoehorn 9–10 billion people into a planet that is already coming apart at the seams'.[3] McKinsey describes the shift as being 'from the supply chain to the supply circle'.[4]

In other chapters, we have discussed how political and economic systems and habits of thought have encouraged short-termism, and impatience for wealth creation – or, in the worst cases, the mere appearance of wealth creation through credit bubbles. This has encouraged households, companies and countries to borrow and consume way beyond their own and the planet's means. Combined with the increasing industrialisation of Asia, Africa and South America, this is putting pressure on the

---

1   Orwell, George, *The Road to Wigan Pier*, Penguin Books, first published Victor Gollanz, 1937.
2   Willard, Bob, *The Sustainability Champion's Guidebook*, New Society Publishers, 2009.
3   Elkington, John, Don't abandon CSR for creating shared value just yet, *Guardian Sustainable Business*, 25 May 2011. Available at: http://www.guardian.co.uk/sustainable-business/sustainability-with-john-elkington/corporate-social-resposibility-creating-shared-value [accessed 28 October 2012].
4   From supply chains to supply circles, McKinsey. Available at: http://www.mckinsey.com/Features/circular_economy [accessed 28 October 2012].

most basic of needs of human life on this fragile planet, including food and water, as discussed in Chapter 2.

Worse, the extreme dysfunctions created by deregulation of global capital (not at all the same thing as a free market), are now accentuating global shortages, as it can become more profitable to store goods than to use them. It is called speculation, and while the theory is that this facilitates free trade, the reality is that it often distorts it.

However, these extreme distortions, and the dangers that they bring, are also fostering innovation. The decoupling of much investment from an understanding of business, focusing instead on speculative activity concerning anticipated price movements, means that business leaders are beginning to voice concern over speculation, and shield themselves from the instability it can bring. Given that such innovation can lead to huge operational savings as well as more sustainable husbandry of finite resources, this pleases the finance director as well as the head of corporate social responsibility.

In the 'old normal', pressure groups and campaigners lobbied big business and the markets to operate sustainably. In the new normal, big business works with pressure groups to innovate smarter, sustainable practices, and seeks to minimise any negative impacts from the markets. This is a seismic change that generates relatively little media coverage.

In 2011, Frank Wienstroth, Howard Schultz and Jorgen Buhl Rasmussen voiced concern over speculation in commodities. Their job titles are, respectively: Spokesman for Purchasing, Supply & Logistics at German car giant BMW; Chief Executive of coffee chain Starbucks, and Chief Executive of the Danish brewery Carlsberg. In the case of BMW, Mr Wienstroth complained that the London metals market has resulted in some 70 per cent of the world's aluminium being warehoused, in the hope of future price rises, meaning that the car manufacturer had to pay a surcharge for supplies to meet its needs. Mr Schultz of Starbucks said in a TV interview:

> *I just think it's inappropriate that there are a group of financial institutions who are somehow orchestrating an unnatural acute rise in commodity prices that ultimately will create a windfall profit for a select few and a significant problem for a whole host of people.*

Mr Rasmussen pointed to the combined effects of climate change and speculation on agricultural supplies for breweries. He said in a media interview:

> *The trigger is clearly a bad harvest, but on top of that you get speculation. Some of the hedge funds, especially those short-selling, I do not see as*

contributing to value creation. Sometimes it's more value-destructive for businesses, but also for the macro-economies'.[5]

When it is impossible to distinguish between the statements of the captains of multinational industry and the heads of anti-poverty and environmental agencies, something major is afoot.

The late twentieth-century agenda, in which green NGOs sought to apply moral or legislative pressure to persuade or force corporations to behave in a more responsible fashion, is out of date. It was based on the assumption that it would cost the organisation to do so, and that resources were effectively infinite in supply. Arguably, such a confrontational dynamic has been counter-productive. By focusing on externalised costs, such as pollution, and arguing – quite understandably – of the unfairness in businesses being able to evade such costs, the belief grew that responsible business always came with a cost. Executives would then naturally run shy of an approach that could lead to reduced margins, market share and possibly even closures and redundancies.

The newest, smartest approaches combine lower environmental impact with savings for the business. Pressure to be lean, smart and green come from within businesses themselves.

INNOVATION

There has been much innovation in supply chain management, where ingenious systems are devised to eke out the 'win–win' where greener, low-impact approaches have an additional benefit of lower business costs and, if not a boost to product quality, at least no impairment. The thriving 2 degrees network for example, (www.2degreesnetwork.com), comprises managers from leading multinational organisations, sharing ideas online and in conferences, about smarter ways of working. The statement of belief on the website states clearly:

Sustainability is increasingly a source of competitive advantage, driving growth, efficiency and profitability. Within years there will be no need to talk about 'sustainable business'. All businesses will be sustainable, or not in business at all.

According to Karin Kreider of the ISEAL Alliance, a non-profit organisation promoting voluntary social and environmental standards, some major companies

---

5   Carlsberg chief calls for hedge fund crackdown, *The Telegraph*, 10 January 2011. Available at: http://www.telegraph.co.uk/finance/businesslatestnews/8249058/Carlsberg-chief-calls-for-hedge-fund-crackdown.html [accessed 16 June 2012].

are starting to address some more hidden risks, such as demographic shifts causing agricultural skills shortages, and political instability. Again, the practical and ethical considerations can coincide, contrasting with conventional economic and political theories which assume they are always in conflict. In the example of cocoa, she says, guaranteeing supply is now a strategic concern for some large consumer brand organisations.

> You have an ageing farmer population – people don't want to work as farmers any more. There is concern that there won't be people to work on farms. There is climate change affecting where you can farm. And political instability in some countries. Cocoa is mostly grown in west Africa. Farms that haven't been kept up, with renovated plant stock, have declining productivity.

Sustainable development, and good prices for farmers, are hugely in the multinationals' interest, in order to keep farmers on the land, maintain productivity, and prevent soil erosion or nutrient depletion. The multinational firms need a radical shift to treat farming skills as a long-term human capital investment. It is also a win–win for farmers, as implementing sustainable practices can help increase productivity and therefore income, prevent soil degradation, maintain water quality, and improve the social conditions for farm workers and their families. 'There is a worry that there won't be a supply in the future', says Ms Kreider. 'This is embedding the need for sustainability. It's not about PR'.

So those making the customary cynical responses to reports about big business adopting a sustainable business strategy as 'green-washing' are often missing the point. 'Green-washing' can be bad for business as well as for the environment; sustainability is not just about preventing resource depletion, it's about corporate survival, and ultimately human survival. Seen in this light, the need to update 'old normal' economic rules of engagement – measurement by quarterly returns, assuming infinite commodity supply, treating people as a disposable resource rather than the core asset – becomes one of pressing as well as profound importance, not something to be deferred to easier times.

Another form of innovation comes in the concept of the sharing economy. Benita Matofska of The People Who Share movement, describes this as an economy based on access rather than ownership, in which production, distribution and consumption are based on sharing. Collaborative Consumption (www.collaborativeconsumption.com) estimates that, in the case of the UK, the sharing economy is worth £22.4 billion, 1.3 per cent of GDP and that it is growing strongly. The global value of the sharing economy could be as high as £330 billion.

Examples include www.airbnb.com, a marketplace for people to book holidays in other people's homes, which has rented more than two million rooms. The car sharing market is booming. In the UK alone, there are estimated to be 100,000 car sharers and the market is predicted to be worth £7.8 billion by 2015.

Businesses such as those listed below offer alternative ways to consume that are based on access rather than ownership:

www.bidandborrow.com
www.ecomodo.com
www.theborrowers.co.uk
www.rentmyitems.com

The movement has also promoted a 'Buy One, Share One'™ (BOSO) concept, a more sustainable concept than the 'Buy One, Get One Free' promotion. BOSO means that at the point of purchase, a product is shared with someone in the local community in need.

'We're taking this to market first in food retail, knowing that the most ethical retailers will see this as a sustainable consumption solution. Ultimately, this can work for fashion and other goods as well as services', says Benita Matofska.

She has also developed the concept of 'corporate shareability' which 'defines an equal relationship from the outset, acknowledging that both parties have something to gain from the partnership – there's shared value. In practice this means that communities and corporations work together for the long term in a reciprocal arrangement with an agreed set of objectives'.[6]

Such innovations are markedly different from the commune experiments common in the 1960s and 1970s, which were more utopian in concept, and more divorced from the mainstream economy. The newer ventures do not ask consumers to opt out, or lower their living standards; rather, it is a consumerist version of the radical shift in corporations from 'take–make–waste' to 'borrow–use–return'.

THE ECONOMICS OF CLIMATE

As noted in Introduction/Chapter 1, debate on climate change has become unfortunately polarised, with much media comment portraying the issue as one involving campaigners who feel that the oceans will start boiling within a few years against those who argue that there is nothing to worry about and nineteenth century-style carbon pollution is good for economic progress. The real issues are more

---

6   See Benita Matofska's blog at the 2degreesnetwork. Available at: http://www.2degrees network.com/groups/employee-engagement/resources/call-yourself-business-future-then-join-sharing-economy_2/ [accessed 18 June 2012].

complex, and they still require urgent attention. To begin with, climate change is already occurring, with phenomena such as a melted glacier in Bolivia affecting the reliability of water supply for irrigation hitting harvests and fisheries. Evo Morales, Bolivia's President and the first head of state to come from the indigenous population, wants polluting countries brought before an international court over the matter.[7]

Other effects are creeping salination of freshwater supplies and loss of arable land in some low-lying oceanic islands, for example Carteret islands and Takuu in the Pacific.[8] Some people have been forced to leave, and migration owing to climate-related loss of water and food supplies could become a significant phenomenon. In eastern Africa, irregular rains have contributed to a food crisis. While this cannot be attributed with absolute certainty to climate change induced by carbon emissions, less regular rainfall has become a pattern in many tropical regions.[9]

Much of the pressure comes from rising human population, and increasingly dense populations on coastal or other vulnerable areas. As with the other aspects described above, this is becoming a business issue in its own right. To take the insurance sector; according to Swiss Re, 2011 was the year with the highest catastrophe-related economic losses in history, at $350 billion, and would have been the costliest year ever for the insurance industry if Japan had been more fully insured.[10] Causes included earthquakes in Japan and New Zealand, floods in Australia and Thailand, and hurricanes and tornadoes in the USA. It is, of course, difficult to be certain whether natural disasters, at least those related to climate, are becoming more common, or whether they are simply affecting more people as the population grows – or both.

This highlights the fragility of many of the world's supply chains. Economic and business changes over the past few decades have featured heavy concentration on specialisation. Global businesses source goods and services from highly specialised 'clusters' of expert providers, located in regions with the skills to support them. It leads to the highest standards, as it can mean that effectively the world's most skilled specialists gather to produce goods and services, and to attract venture capital for

7   Bolivian villagers want compensation as glaciers melt, BBC news, 19 April 2010. Available at: http://news.bbc.co.uk/1/hi/world/americas/8629379.stm [accessed 28 October 2012].

8   The real and predicted effect of sea level rise, Ecology Global Network online article, 5 March 2012. Available at: http://www.ecology.com/2012/03/05/effects-sea-level-rise/ [accessed 28 October 2012].

9   East Africa drought remains huge crisis, BBC news, 20 October 2011. Available at: http://www.bbc.co.uk/news/world-africa-15380244 [accessed 28 October 2012].

10   Estimates by Swiss Re Sigma team. See: Sigma – preliminary estimates for 2011: Natural catastrophes and man-made disasters caused economic losses of USD 350 billion and cost insurers USD 108 billion. Available at: http://www.swissre.com/media/news_releases/nr_20111215_preliminary_estimates_2011.html [accessed 28 October 2012].

innovative ideas that such groupings can generate. It also makes logistical sense, but does create obvious vulnerabilities in supply, as a major earthquake or drought could cause serious disruptions in manufactured or agricultural products. The 2011 Japanese earthquake affected supplies to car companies around the world, for example, affecting economic growth.

This calls for smart thinking; that 'just in time' management supply systems and specialised clusters need to incorporate some forms of contingency that might appear to reduce efficiency in 'normal' conditions, on the pragmatic assumption that 'normal' conditions do not continue in perpetuity.

GOVERNMENTS ARE LAGGING

Another radical shift necessary is to spread the concept of political and economic leadership to all institutions, not just governments. In the case of adapting to the new normal, the innovative companies and enterprises summarised in this chapter can inspire and encourage others, leading to a more optimistic agenda than the old normal of attritional lobbying, reluctant law-making and erratic enforcement. The traditional approach consists of NGOs lobbying governments to pass binding legislation to force companies to reduce environmental damage or uphold labour standards, often agreed at time-consuming expensive global summits, producing agreements that end up being watered down to something that everyone can agree with.

As companies and other enterprises, such as shared economy initiatives, show the way, leadership can be spread. Protecting the environment and improving working conditions become a shared, sustainable, profitable goal, not a tiresome bureaucratic regulation imposed on unwilling participants. This is not to argue against summits or regulation; rather it is to place such activity as being one among a range of initiatives, in which treaties and laws form but part of a range of initiatives, and are optimised, rather than maximised.

In this new normal, the agreements at the United Nations climate change summit in Durban in 2011, and at the Rio+20 summit held in mid-2012, become platforms for further innovation to mutual advantage, not grudgingly implemented minimum activities for reluctant participants. In addition to legally binding commitments, which will not come into force until 2020, a Durban working group will begin to work next year developing 'mitigation, adaptation, finance, technology development and transfer, transparency of action and support and capacity building'. To those who see binding rules as the only route to progress, this looks like a fudge and a disappointment – and there is a risk that the hopes will be disappointed. The energy and innovation in corporate shareability and similar initiatives, however, show that the Durban working group could represent a significant opportunity.

In March 2012, for example, the consumer products company Unilever announced more programmes as part of its moves towards being a more sustainable business. It published details of a range of research projects in the areas of waste, water and health. This forms part of the 'Open Innovation' initiative, in which potential collaborators are invited to work with the firm's research & development team to develop innovations.

Open Innovation director Roger Leech said:

> Smart collaboration with partners gives both parties the freedom to do business in new and invigorating ways – creating shared value along the way. It brings together the expertise and experience of our sustainable innovation capability with new thinking and creativity from partners, creating new business models in which ideas flourish.

Key areas of focus include technologies which bring safe water to poor communities, and the development of lighter and more environmentally friendly packaging. It is also looking to develop laundry products that can be used at lower temperatures and use less water.

THE PATH OF CONVERSATIONS

There is increasing evidence that human communities – whether they are companies, trade unions, villages or nations – follow the path of their conversations. This is why politicians search for the 'narrative' – the description or interpretation of events that holds sway for the bulk of the population. It may be broadly true or dangerously misleading or oversimplified, but humans understand the world through stories, especially shared stories. This is a powerful insight. The discipline of 'appreciative inquiry', pioneered in the 1980s by David Cooperrider and Suresh Srivastva, encourages us to begin positive conversations, based on the understanding that we can learn more from what we do well than from our mistakes.[11] For the same reason, it is essential the business leaders pay as much attention to their beliefs, relationships and communications as to the strategic positioning of the company (see Chapter 7 'Conscious Leadership'); also that economics moves towards a behavioural understanding, away from faith in 'laws' of markets or social classes that are based on inaccurate metaphors based on the physical sciences, rather than actual observation of human society.

---

11   The seminal work is *Appreciative Inquiry into Organizational Life*, written and published by David Cooperrider and Suresh Srivastva, 1987. There is much written and other material on Appreciative Inquiry. See http://appreciativeinquiry.case.edu/ [accessed 28 October 2012].

Also, for this reason, we have chosen positive case studies for this book; to illustrate the art of the possible. It is necessary to expose exploitation, cruelty and corruption in economic affairs, but this is never a complete analysis, and there is a risk of dwelling too long on such evils, and subtly inviting them to be repeated. The danger of the self-fulfilling prophesy tends to be overlooked in the more cynical approaches to economics and politics.

IN SUMMARY

The supply circle, or corporate shareability, or shared value, are not mere soundbites, but proven methods of meeting disparate human needs without damaging others. There is now a thriving network of corporate sustainability specialists, and increasing awareness of how environmentally smarter supply systems can actually help the business and the customer.

CONCLUSION

This is not an interesting book. We shall seek to challenge praise from those who declare it 'interesting' but who baulk at the implications. We're saying that almost everything about the way in which work and the organisation and the leadership task and politics are viewed is fundamentally awry and needs rethinking. We're not offering a mere interesting aside; we're saying pretty much everything has to change – while recognising the pioneering business leaders who have begun to do this already.

Of course, we may be wrong, and we would welcome debate. If we are wrong, we are wrong in a big way and you can pretty much ignore everything we've written. But if we are broadly right, then the implication is an overhaul not just of governance structures and leadership skills, but of reporting systems for businesses and investors; the way in which politics is understood and reported on; the priorities of major news media; the role of the leader in commerce and politics.

We are perfectly aware that this claim is going to sound overambitious, perhaps even arrogant. We did not set out to be. We are at times daunted, almost embarrassed, by the scale of the implications that we have stumbled upon while working with organisational leaders, or writing about organisational leadership. The evidence and experience we have accumulated over the years point to implications that stretch far beyond the boardroom. They indicate that some of the core, unspoken beliefs behind the way in which we run organisations and economies, and the most influential beliefs that inform them, are fundamentally mistaken. We have, almost accidentally, entered territory that demands deep inquiry and new thought across a range of subjects on which we acknowledge we are not experts; so we encourage wider discussion and inquiry, and have signalled some of the writers and speakers we would recommend – though doubtless there will be many, many others.

Corporate social responsibility is an area that has traditionally been the recipient of token, often patronising, attitudes. Too many corporations have regarded it as a matter of a few charity donations and superficial initiatives, handily combined with a photo opportunity for the chairman. Trade unions have been dismissive, regarding such endeavours as peripheral to their struggle for what they assume are greater gains for the worker through collective struggle and lobbying for statutory rights.

Thousands, perhaps millions, of individuals in recent decades have begun their career campaigning for a worthwhile social or environmental improvement while on their gap year or in their first job, then moved to a corporation when starting a family and needing a better or more reliable income. Typically, this is viewed as 'selling out', and it is assumed that, in making this move, the individual has given up hope of working for a better society and abandoned their principles.

But what if they didn't?

What if this Cinderella – social responsibility, shared value, whichever label you prefer – grows to become a dominant force, doing more to overcome poverty, discrimination and environmental damage than any other single movement? What is stopping it? We would argue, nothing but superstition and the age-old belief, shared by old-style managers and trade unionists, that social responsibility is bad for business; a belief we now know to be false. From this simple recognition, momentous change can follow.

A natural advantage of corporate social responsibility managers is a tendency to focus on practical, but also optimistic, objectives. This is in contrast with many non-corporate social and environmental campaigners who have a tendency to project images of doom – especially about prospects for the climate – and hatred of the forces of capitalism. This creates a climate of fear, which can cause potential supporters to feel disengagement or impotence. Progressive change has never been effected through fear. Martin Luther King did not promise vengeance upon lynch mobs. He had a dream. Nelson Mandela did not pledge to drive the white folk of out South Africa. He promised equality.

Green campaigners in particular have to learn from this. They must pay attention to the psychological climate, as well as the weather, and learn from successful campaigns. An unlikely positive change can become possible, and sometimes quite rapidly, but only by harnessing hope and offering practical solutions. If you threaten the species with extinction, don't be surprised if no one listens. If green campaigners have nothing to offer but misanthropy, misery and the hair shirt, they will fail to engage people. Just as the workers' misery does not create profits, there is nothing inevitable about ecological degradation in producing comfort and joy to human beings. Human civilisation, and profit-making businesses and the products and services that they create, are not some form of pollution upon the earth. Now, businesses may create pollution, or waste, or discrimination, or exploitation, but equally they may choose to eliminate such horrors. The choice is up to us.

INDEX

If you have found this book useful you may be interested in other titles from Gower

The Rise and Fall of Management

A Brief History of Practice, Theory and Context

Gordon Pearson

Hardback: 978-0-566-08976-3

Paperback: 978-1-4094-4829-7

e-book: 978-0-566-08977-0

The Road to Co-operation

Escaping the Bottom Line

Gordon Pearson

Hardback: 978-1-4094-3202-9

Paperback: 978-1-4094-4830-3

e-book: 978-1-4094-3203-6

The Failure and the Future of Accounting

Strategy, Stakeholders, and Business Value

David Hatherly

Hardback: 978-1-4094-5354-3

e-book: 978-1-4094-5355-0

GOWER

Choosing Leaders and Choosing to Lead

Science, Politics and Intuition in Executive Selection

Douglas Board

Hardback: 978-1-4094-3648-5

e-book: 978-1-4094-3649-2

Third Generation Leadership and the Locus of Control

Knowledge, Change and Neuroscience

Douglas G. Long

Hardback: 978-1-4094-4453-4

e-book: 978-1-4094-4454-1

Managing Responsibly

Alternative Approaches to Corporate Management and Governance

Edited by Jane Buckingham and Venkataraman Nilakant

Hardback: 978-1-4094-2745-2

e-book: 978-1-4094-2746-9